Praise for **Exemplary Leadership I**

"Dr. Peter Litchka has produced an outstanding resource for all school administrators. He has used historical figures to illustrate how professional educators can and must learn from the past. New and experienced administrators will find this book both practical and inspirational." —**John W. Hunt**, PhD, associate professor emeritus

"In line with the notion stating there is much wisdom in practices, this powerful book offers leaders a genuine and insightful perspective on their professional conduct. Using historical examples from great leaders as reference, it brings current school leaders' stories which tackle the essence of educational leadership. This book offers useful insights for school leaders and a port for their self-reflective journeys. Great book!" —**Adam Nir**, professor, Educational Administration Policy and Leadership, The School of Education, The Hebrew University of Jerusalem

"Today's issues facing current school leaders appear insurmountable. Litchka's book addresses these issues in a practical, easy to understand but yet with deep profound meaning. The insight and helpful advice is presented in a measured mix of systematic research and anecdotal evidence providing school leaders regardless of experience, a valuable resource. School related Issues are no longer inseparable and this book shows why. School leaders will see their reality reflected in these pages through a healthy dose of real life scenarios, with added value of practical grounding reflections on how to deal with the challenges of the role. This book is written by someone 'who has been there' and designed to help prepare you now and for the years ahead. It's a book to help you understand yourself, and how you and your work connect through the inescapable medium of contemporary leadership." —**Frank F. Calzi**, PhD, retired chairperson school leadership, Niagara University, New York

"Information provided in this work presents a unique look at the leadership experiences of individual practitioners and include a discussion of these experiences. The discussions, in addition to dealing with traditional subjects, present topics such as, physical fitness, reflecting on emotional self-awareness, interacting with others, and guidance on how to improve readiness through external activities beyond the job. A nice read that blends actual leadership together with theory; a helpful read." —**Robert H. Beach**, PhD, retired former dean; professor; and executive director of the National Council of Professors of Educational Administration

"As a former superintendent of two rural school districts, I understand very well the balance needed to stay ahead of the day-to-day business of running the district, and the necessity of providing guidance and leadership to the members of the board of education and administrative team. Too often, the former trumps the latter as all involved are being pulled in a multitude of directions. I found that book studies were a perfect way to engage all in meaningful conversations about educational leadership and institutional integrity. How I would have loved to have had Dr. Litchka's book available to me during my tenure as a school superintendent! His approach of relating the tenets of leadership to great leaders in history, and then providing a parallel story from current practitioners in the field of educational leadership, is brilliant. This book is readable and relevant...a must-read for anyone considering a career as a leader in an educational setting. Kudos!" —**Christine J. Tibbetts**, retired school superintendent, New York State

Exemplary Leadership Practices

Exemplary Leadership Practices

Learning from the Past to Enhance Future School Leadership

Peter R. Litchka

ROWMAN & LITTLEFIELD
Lanham • Boulder • New York • London

Published by Rowman & Littlefield
A wholly owned subsidiary of The Rowman & Littlefield Publishing Group, Inc.
4501 Forbes Boulevard, Suite 200, Lanham, Maryland 20706
www.rowman.com

Unit A, Whitacre Mews, 26-34 Stannary Street, London SE11 4AB

British Library Cataloguing in Publication Information Available

Library of Congress Cataloging-in-Publication Data

ISBN 978-1-4758-1966-3 (cloth : alk. paper) -- ISBN 978-1-4758-1967-0 (pbk. : alk. paper) -- ISBN 978-1-4758-1968-7 (electronic)

♾ ™ The paper used in this publication meets the minimum requirements of American National Standard for Information Sciences Permanence of Paper for Printed Library Materials, ANSI/NISO Z39.48-1992.

Printed in the United States of America

I dedicate this book to Don Vetter, who has been my supervisor, mentor, colleague and friend. Don has inspired me, challenged me, and empowered me. There is no way I would ever be where I am today without his support and friendship. I am truly a lucky man! Thanks, Don!

Contents

Foreword

Harry Truman once said,

> While still a boy I could see that history had some extremely valuable lessons to teach. I learned from it that a leader is a man who has the ability to get other people to do what they don't want to do, and like it.

Peter Litchka's book, *Exemplary Leadership Practices: Learning from the Past to Enhance Future School Leadership*, provides the reader with insightful opportunities to reflect about different leadership styles and approaches. This book presents a well-organized historical analysis of the experiences of leaders who made positive impacts on their respective societies by virtue of their leadership acumen and behavioral dispositions. He correlates those historical experiences with the contemporary experiences of "real world" educational leaders who have experienced similar situations in various settings.

Litchka uses unique historical figures and pragmatic contemporary examples to teach powerful leadership lessons. He clearly and poignantly illustrates that whether overturning colonial oppression, forming a new nation, forging a global organization, or administering a school building or school district, leadership is truly the ability to get other people to do what they don't want to do, and like it!

This book not only captures the essence of what Truman was suggesting but also reminds the reader that meaningful and sustainable leadership success is possible but requires continuous learning, acute vigilance, and creative approaches by the leader to motivate followers to accomplish goals that they may not have initially believed realistic or rewarding.

Litchka selects an interesting array of personalities to study in the various chapters of the book. Each of those leaders manifested leadership characteristics and behavioral dispositions for leading organizations that reflect the key leadership concepts espoused by Mark Twain's perspective of the Mississippi River boat pilot when he identified

> two things seemed pretty apparent to me. One was, that in order to be a Mississippi River pilot a man had got to learn more than any one man ought to be allowed to know; and the other was, that he must learn it all over again in a different way every 24 hours.

Accordingly, effective school leaders need to know more about the people, things, and ideas of their respective micro context, including themselves, and the macro and mega contexts of their organization, than any one person ought to know, and they must learn it all over again every day since the metaphorical turbulent currents of leadership rivers are constantly changing!

Litchka appropriately integrates that concept into each of the chapters of this book by using historical figures, contemporary examples, and related research references as well as sage practical advice. It is a captivating read because the leadership stories are uniquely developed with a historian's deft touch, a sociologist's impactful orientation, a psychologist's analytical focus, and a teacher's acute desire to make the lessons interesting and meaningful. Litchka synthesizes the key leadership attributes and actions of the varied leaders chronicled in this book into a grand leadership scheme that reinforces several imperative leadership lessons that all practicing and aspiring leaders need to know, including the lessons of historical figures such as Woodrow Wilson, Mustafa Kemal (Ataturk), Mohandas Gandhi, Charles Dickens, and Golda Meir.

While Litchka teaches the reader about effective leaders and their approaches to accomplishing their goals, he also evaluates the personal cost to them to do so. He clearly demonstrates via his different stories examples that leadership is all about vision, relationships, passion, fortitude, humility, modeling, and risk taking. Each of his chapters provide the reader with interesting historical experiences of the selected leader, the social nature of the context, as well as the personal leadership interactions and self-reflections that facilitated or negatively impacted the leader's accomplishments.

Enjoy the history lessons of this book, and you will be able to reflect about these on your own leadership principles, practices, and value. You will learn much about being a successful leader from Peter Litchka's wisdom and research, and you will be more satisfied and more successful because you did!

Walter S. Polka, EdD

Preface

There is no greater agony than bearing an untold story inside you.
—Maya Angelou

During my research for this book, a superintendent asked me to attend a regional meeting of superintendents. These meetings were held monthly and chaired by a different superintendent each month. There were close to fifty school superintendents in the room. The person in charge—the superintendent who invited me—after a few welcoming remarks asked the group to put their pens down, shut down their cell phones and laptops, and then, close their eyes. She then asked them to think about an event that, as a school leader, "shook them to their core"—good or bad. She asked them to take a few minutes and think about this event. She then broke them into groups of about seven or eight, and said:

> Now, I want you to tell the story. Don't leave anything out. Share your thoughts, your feelings, what you learned, what you wish you had done better (or differently). There are no rules except only one person can speak at a time, no one can take notes, and everyone must make eye contact with the storyteller. Each teller has ten minutes to tell the story. The most important thing, though, is to speak from the heart and share this story.

For the next hour and a half, these stories became the language of leadership for the participants. There were smiles and tears, moments of silence, and even a few cheers along the way. Some laughs were heard, but not many. With the exception of the storyteller at each table, there was no noise in the room. Everyone—storyteller and listeners—were paying attention.

It was clear that the storyteller was gaining much from this experience: an opportunity to share an event that perhaps was never shared before, especially in "public." At the same time, the listeners were hearing stories that may have been similar to what they had experienced, or hearing something that perhaps was not imaginable. These stories communicated who each person was, what was valued, disseminated shared knowledge was, and provided a reference point to the future. Stories became the currency for school leadership that day, and I can't imagine those who participated ever forgetting what they heard.

After leaving this meeting, I began to think about the powerful learning that took place in that room. Real stories shared in a way that was personal and the basis for deep learning and reflecting. Thus, the basis of this book began as a quest to have school leaders[1] share their stories and learn from each other as well.

Yet at the same time, leadership stories from outside of the educational context can be as powerful. So as I read notes from interviews over the past ten years and listened to new stories from school leaders, it became evident to me that great leaders from history have a story (or many stories) to tell that could help contemporary school leaders in dealing with the myriad of issues they face on a daily basis. In addition, these historical figures provide a model that a school leader might wish to consider.

The examples given in this book include historical leaders from around the world, from different eras and from distinct positions of leadership as well. History, to some, is a collection of stories about people, places, and events. Today we live in a highly interconnected world in which the actions of people, and where and how things happen, can have a significant impact beyond borders and across oceans. An event that takes place in Paris, or Beirut, or Mumbai, or even New York City now reaches the world in seconds, when in the past it might have taken hours or even days for the rest of the world to read or hear about it.

As the world continues along the course of more and faster is better, could we be losing sight of what has happened in the past, and the lessons from which we learn? Certainly, the environmental condition of the earth comes to mind, as does the current geopolitical status of the world. To some, the answers are simple: it is best to not look to the past in attempting to resolve current situations; otherwise, we are doomed to the same types of failed policy.

Yet we need to continue to learn from the past. A full understanding of how great leaders provided leadership can be very helpful for not only current policymakers in education but also for scholars and practitioners of leadership. The present nature and complexity of leadership is heavily dependent on the past, as we cannot fully understand or appreciate the current context without going back and exploring the past.

Exemplary leadership from the past can cross cultures and contexts. Learning how others from the past were successful—or unsuccessful—in dealing with the issues of a particular time can help contemporary and aspiring leaders to contextualize leadership in general, and to their current condition as well. To ignore the leadership of greats such as Alexander the Great, Abraham Lincoln, Mohandas Gandhi, Martin Luther King, Golda Meir, and many others would run the risk of having leaders, including those in education, not completely knowing, understanding, appreciating, and applying exemplary lessons from the past to today's educational leadership environment.

Rudyard Kipling once said, "If history were taught in the forms of stories, it would never be forgotten."[2] Over the past decade, I, along with a number of colleagues, have listened to the stories of many school leaders—superintendents and principals, mostly. Some of the stories were happy, some sad. Some of the leaders cried when they shared the stories. Others would roll their eyes or, after telling the story, would sit in silence. Some would even laugh.

But one thing that came from each story was that by sharing it, the leader was sharing a very deep and personal part of his or her history of school leadership.

Such stories help us to understand the values, beliefs, and morals of contemporary school leaders; they help us define what it means to be a leader in the contemporary context of school leadership in America. Yet far too often, stories are told and soon forgotten, or not told at all. We can learn history in terms of stories, either through telling them or listening to the stories of others. But it is more than telling and listening. It is learning, for not only those who wish to be school leaders but also for those who currently are in positions of school leadership.

PLAN OF THE BOOK

The book has five main chapters, each with an introduction, overview of theory, a historical account of leadership, a story from a practicing school leader, and a conclusion called Learning for Leading.

The first chapter, *Temet Nosce* (Know Thyself), looks at leadership from the inside—those personal and individual values and beliefs that are critical for success. For the historical account, Woodrow Wilson's plight as a senator from New Jersey in taking on the political bosses of that state is presented. The story of a school superintendent, who has based his success on the wrong kind of values, ultimately leading to his downfall, provides a lesson on values that all leaders may wish to consider.

Chapter 2, *The Magic Behind the Meaning*, argues how important symbolic leadership can be to the success of a school leader. Symbols arrive in all shapes and forms, and can have a significant impact on how followers and others view the ability of the leader to lead! From the historical perspective,

Mustafa Kemal (Ataturk) and Mohandas Gandhi are presented in terms of how symbols and leadership can provide and exemplify a basis for moving followers to places they have never been before. In addition, a story of a school principal who models symbolic leadership in turning around a high school that has seen better times is presented.

The dilemma of school leadership and change is presented in chapter 3, *From Chrysalis to Butterfly*. While there have been numerous books on leading change, this chapter provides a perspective on the personal side of leading change, which includes courage, self-sacrifice, persistence, and lack of ego. Once again, Mohandas Gandhi, this time in South Africa as a young lawyer trying to support Indians living under the oppression of the British Colonial Office. Also presented is the story of a female high school principal who leads a significant and successful change effort, in spite of many obstacles.

In the busy and hectic life of the contemporary school leader, time to think is often relegated to the status of "I'll get to that as soon as the next crisis is resolved." Unfortunately, the crises never seem to end, and quality thinking keeps getting pushed aside for many school leaders. Thus, reflection and leadership is the theme for chapter 4, *Thinking About Thinking*. As will be suggested in the chapter, perhaps contemporary leaders need to be thinking more and doing less! In this chapter, a leader in the field of nineteenth-century literature has found himself at the mercy of the publishers to write, write, and write even more!

It is only when this author begins to immerse himself into observing, thinking, and reflecting does he emerge from this fatigue and taxing way of life. The story of a principal who sees not only herself but staff as well on a "treadmill going nowhere" is presented in terms of how to get the entire faculty of a school "to slow down and think"; "thinking about thinking" becomes the mantra for the entire school.

Chapter 5, *Surviving and Thriving*, looks at some of the negative issues facing superintendents, including female superintendents (who are often faced with their own set of unique issues), and how such leaders can not only get up after being knocked down (in many cases, multiple times) but also how they can become stronger and more effective as a leader. From the historical vantage, the account of the first female prime minister of a Western democracy is presented. The story of a female superintendent, facing the trauma of a board of education acting in both an unethical and sexist manner, provides a glimpse of leadership and resiliency during very difficult times. [3]

The last chapter, *Looking Back—and Ahead*, offers some final thoughts in terms of advice, encouragement, inspiration, and a final story as well. It is my hope these will help school leaders as they successfully maneuver through the sometimes challenging but always fulfilling and rewarding world of contemporary school leadership.

Acknowledgments

Since coming into higher education a decade ago, I have had numerous opportunities to collaborate in various teaching and scholarly pursuits with Dr. Walter (Walt) Polka of Niagara University. We knew each other growing up in the LaSalle section of Niagara Falls and had similar career paths (social studies teacher, coach, building and district leadership). But it was in 2004 in which we met up again in Statesboro, Georgia, for dinner. From that point, we began to collaborate. Walt became my mentor and opened numerous doors for me, such as "Hey, Pete, want to go to Turkey to a conference?" "Whaddya think about this idea for a paper?" or "Pete, let's write a book!" Getting to the point of writing my own book would never have happened without Walt's guidance, modeling of best practices, occasional prodding, and of course, his friendship. I acknowledge Walt for all that he has given to me as a mentor and friend. Here's hoping that Walt and I live long enough to see the Buffalo Bills win a Super Bowl!

Thanks to my friends and colleagues at Loyola University Maryland: Mickey Fenzel, Peter Rennert-Ariev, Vic Delclos, and Joshua Smith. In their own way, they each have provided support, encouragement, and mentoring for me in the writing of this book, as well as other scholarship in which I have been involved.

And thanks to the school leaders across America and the world, who have shared their stories with me. Being a school leader in the twenty-first century is most challenging, to say the least, but without great leaders, our schools will drift and be the target of the latest and greatest ways to improve teaching and learning. Here's to the next generation of school leaders who can and will stand strong for what schools, teaching, and learning are really about!

Chapter One

Temet Nosce (Know Thyself)

It's said that one day, Frederick the Great of Prussia was walking on the outskirts of Berlin when he encountered a very old man walking ramrod straight in the opposite direction.

"Who are you?" Frederick asked his subject.

"I am a king," replied the old man.

"A king!" laughed Frederick. "Over what kingdom do you reign?"

"Over myself," was the proud old man's reply.

THE INNER CORE

Sometimes when we look in the mirror, we like what we see. Perhaps we have lost some weight. Or bought some new clothes that look very good on us. Or maybe, that gray hair doesn't look so bad after all.

Other times, though, when we look in the mirror, it's not so pleasurable. Maybe we have put on some weight. Or that favorite sweater doesn't look as good as it once did. Perhaps we have gotten older and didn't notice the lines under our eyes until now.

So when leaders look in the mirror, what do they see? For some, they may see someone who needs to get things done now, worries about the present with little thought of the future, tries to be collaborative and yet, at the same time, be decisive and in charge! This can be found not only in the offices and boardrooms of Fortune 500 companies that are concerned with profits, stock prices, and earnings but in schools as well. Superintendents and principals are under more pressure now than ever "to just get those test scores up," to keep the budget under control, and by all means, make sure the board of education knows everything about everyone everywhere.

Other leaders may see something different. They see someone who is passionate yet deliberate in their leadership. They see someone who is concerned about both the present and the future, and looks at leadership as a journey, not a series of unrelated events. Profits and earnings are important to corporations, as test scores and finances are to schools. But they are not the only things that are important. In the case of education, leadership balances out the pressure of the now with a constant dialogue focusing on what students need to know, understand, and be able to do when they leave.

So why the difference? Many leaders, especially in education, would love nothing more than to be a real leader in every sense of the definition, but unfortunately, they are anchored in the pressure of now. Within this context, such leaders are expected to have all the answers, solve all the problems (and quickly), and be in control at all times (Great Man Theory). In addition, this type of leader is likely to feel that it is safer to manage (do things right) than to actually lead (do the right thing for the right reasons) and take some risks along the way.

The perception found within this paradigm is primarily based upon winning and losing (success or failure), with little or no room for deviation. Thus, the former is less likely to take chances, more likely to avoid failure, and more likely to make decisions based upon previous successes (whatever worked before should work now). Then, it is on to the next problem(s) to be solved.

It is much safer to lead in this manner—at least for a while. In this type of leadership, organizational charts can be developed, goals and strategies created and implemented, and benchmarks (a favorite expression in education) can be established. From this, formal assessments can occur regarding the effectiveness of people and programs.

It stands to reason that in education, many underperforming school districts and schools often search for this type of leadership, in hope of showing stakeholders progress that will be accomplished in a methodical, linear manner. And in order to do this in such schools, the teachers and students are recipients of scripted curriculum programs that aim for proficiency, and unfortunately, do not target areas of critical thinking, creativity, and holistic learning.

The irony of this is that all one needs to do is peruse vacancy announcements for superintendents or principals. Leadership descriptors such as *collaborative*, *visionary*, *change agent*, and *people person* are but a few that are found in the advertisements. However, it doesn't take much time in many instances for the leader to discover that this type of leadership is not what was really wanted; instead, they want a manager-leader.

Furthermore, some contemporary school leaders may think that leadership is all about telling others what to do—since I am the superintendent of schools (or school principal), my authority will convince others that my ideas must be followed because I am the leader. But as we know, leading others is much more than just doing what the leader says. Leadership is building relationships, seeing the big picture, and influencing others toward a common goal. But just like looking in the mirror, most of us—including leaders—do not look at ourselves realistically. Most of the time, we see what we want to see and avoid the other unpleasant views that may be staring at us.

Why, then, can't leaders, especially within the contemporary educational context, lead in a manner that is more of a journey and less of an event? Contemporary society can be impatient, and may ask of the school leader, "What have you done for me lately?" First and foremost, this kind of leadership takes time. It takes time to learn about the school and community, as well as the staff and students. Collaboration, shared decision making, and other leadership behaviors are based upon getting everyone involved in the journey.

When we study the lives of great leaders throughout history—from Caesar to Alexander the Great to Lincoln to Gandhi to Mandela—these are people who have changed the world during their lifetime and well beyond. These very special people, from a distance, would appear to have certain characteristics that perhaps the rest of us do not have, or have not yet discovered. They might appear to be stronger, wiser, more disciplined, more strategic, more creative, and so on. These leaders also knew themselves and what they deeply valued and believed in—they understood and acted upon their inner core.

While a leader may have the ability to be positive and optimistic, strategic and decisive, and collaborative and visionary, success will be very difficult to reach and maintain if a strong inner core of beliefs and values is not supported. If the inner core is missing or has not been discovered, the results could be a leader—who happens to be a really good person—who has become isolated, angry, fearful, or exhausted, both physically and emotionally.

Over the past several decades, a significant amount of attention has been focused on leadership from the inside out, which suggests the need for a leader to know oneself before trying to lead others. Understanding oneself can be a tool for successful leadership in that it provides the leader with the ability to identify and balance strengths with weaknesses, using and modeling this practice when providing leadership. In addition, relationships built upon trust, openness, and respect will be developed between the leader and followers.

Consider what others have suggested about the nature of understanding one's self:

He who knows others is wise. He who knows himself is enlightened.
—Lao Tzu (570–490 BC)

What we think, we become.   All that we are arises with our thoughts.   With
our thoughts, we make the world. —The Buddha (563–483 BC)

If you know the enemy and know yourself you need not fear the results of a
hundred battles.
—Sun Tzu (544–496 BC)

No one can give you better advice than yourself. —Cicero (106–43 BC)

This above all, to thine own self, be true.
—William Shakespeare (1564–1616)

Search others for their virtues, thyself for thy vices.
—Benjamin Franklin (1706–1790)

Nothing can bring you peace but yourself. —Ralph Waldo Emerson
(1803–1882)

The cave you fear to enter holds the treasure you seek.
—Joseph Campbell (1904–1987)

What is necessary to change a person is to change his awareness of himself.
—Abraham H. Maslow (1908–1970)

To be authentic is literally to be your own author, to discover your own native
energies and desires, and then to find your own way of acting on them.
—Warren G. Bennis (1925–2014)

The first person we need to examine is ourselves.
—John Maxwell (1947–)

One of the most acclaimed proponents of this concept was Stephen Covey
(1932–2012). In 1989, he published *The 7 Habits of Highly Effective People*,
which became a worldwide success in not only book sales but also in having
thousands of organizations, including schools, adopt the tenets of his philosophy. Covey's *7 Habits* are for the individual to be proactive, to begin with the
end in mind, put first things first, think win-win, seek first to understand and
then be understood, synergize, and sharpen the saw.

In order for an individual to become successful in attaining self-actualiza-
tion, the individual must align oneself to what Covey calls "true north,"
which become the foundation of how one acts and leads (habits). By practicing and acting upon these habits, an individual can move from dependence to
independence to interdependence and onto continuous improvement.

Covey then used this framework to focus on successful leadership.

In *Principle-Centered Leadership* (1990), Covey suggested specific steps for the leader to center one's leadership through the use of four dimensions of the "leadership compass": security, guidance, wisdom, and power within the organization. Covey dedicates an entire section of the book, Finding Your Voice, in which he strongly posits that once the seven habits have been internalized and acted upon, the individual, upon becoming a leader, will have the ability to influence followers by exhibiting leadership attributes that will help both the leader and the followers experience life like never before. According to Covey,

> These four words—vision, discipline, passion and conscience—essentially embody many, many other characteristics used to describe those traits we associate with people whose influence [leadership] is great, whether known to many or few. [1]

Covey published *The 8th Habit: From Effectiveness to Greatness* (2004), in which he continued to focus on people (leaders) finding their inner core, and then helping others (followers) do the same. Being a great leader, according to Covey, includes modeling the seven habits, finding "one voice" through shared visioning and alignment of common values, ensuring that both personal and organizational values and strategies are in alignment, and that leaders need to consistently find opportunities to empower everyone within the organization. However, without knowing one's own voice, it will be difficult, if not impossible, to lead one's self or others to success.

James Kouzes and Barry Posner (1987) first published *The Leadership Challenge*, in which they proposed that there are certain practices and behaviors that can significantly help a leader achieve greatness. Based upon research garnered from around the world and across many different industries and professions, Kouzes and Posner offered the following practices: Model the Way, Inspire a Shared Vision, Challenge the Process, Enable Others to Act, and Encourage the Heart. [2]

The first of these practices—Model the Way—describes how leaders identify (or even discover) their own personal beliefs and values, and act upon such in how they will lead, treat, and interact with others within the organization. In clarifying their own beliefs and values, Kouzes and Posner suggest leaders must find their own voice first, share their voice with others, and create a climate of shared voices. Shared values and beliefs can help a leader develop a culture of trust, loyalty, and sense of direction. Without such shared voices, the leader will have difficulty leading others to optimal results, especially during difficult times that may include the ever-daunting process of "changing the way we do things around here."

In addition to clarifying values and beliefs, the authors suggest that leaders need to be the example for others to follow. Values and belief statements that are not acted upon in a regular, consistent, and deliberate manner will have little meaning to the organization. How many times have we been told by leaders to "do what I say, not what I do"?

In order to be meaningful, the leader must embody these principles in all aspects of their role as leader, so that everyone in the organization knows exactly what these principles are, how to act upon them, and if in question, watch how the leader models such principles. Lee Bolman and Terrence Deal in *Leading with Soul: An Uncommon Journey of Spirit* (1995) used a contemporary parable as the backdrop of the book to contend that finding one's own soul is the essence of successful leadership, particularly within the contemporary context of modern society. Bolman and Deal suggest:

> Each of us has a special contribution to make if we can shoulder the personal and spiritual work needed to discover and share our own gifts. Across sectors and levels, organizations are starved for the leadership they need. Leaders who have lost touch with their souls, who are confused and uncertain about their core values, inevitably lose their way or sound an uncertain trumpet. [3]

Accordingly, the authors suggest that what is often missing in leadership and within the organizations is soul and spirit. In such situations, the leader and/or the followers have failed to discover their inner core, beliefs, and values. Or in some circumstances, the core has been discovered but not acted upon. And ironically, success can occur, at least temporarily.

At some point, this lack of a common voice can take a heavy toll on both the leader and followers, causing a marked decline in creativity, work ethic, loyalty, and ultimately performance.

Bolman and Deal submit that a most critical role of any leader in any type of environment is to instill spirit, zest, and life within the organization. And the first step in accomplishing this is for the leader himself or herself to search and find meaning in their own life—both personal and professional—and once this is accomplished, enable others to do the same. By doing this, each will begin to live a life of passion and purpose to a much higher level than before.

In addition, Bolman and Deal suggest that such soulful leaders become leaders who gift (not give). To gift is to offer one's spirit, soul, and passion to others—with no strings attached! Genuine gifting can transform a school from a dreary place where one has to be (e.g., principal, teacher, student) to a place where one wants to be. The gifting by the leader of authorship, love, power, and significance is critical in the quest toward collective efficacy, wisdom, and spirit.

However, leaders cannot gift something that they don't have or don't know they have. Nor can they lead others to places where they have never experienced.

There are few examples of successes in educational leadership literature using such models. And a chief reason is that in most, if not all, cases there was little if any genuine, soulful leadership. Sadly, such schools and school districts fall further behind, where disappointment and cynicism become the norm. According to Bolman and Deal,

> To prevail in the face of our spiritual challenges, we need a vision of leadership rooted in an enduring sense of human wisdom. We need a new generation of seekers who have the courage to confront their own demons, to embark upon a personal quest for spirit and heart, and the commitment to share their learning and gifts with others. [4]

If one were to follow the wisdom of Bolman and Deal, school leaders should thoroughly know and understand their own spirit and soul; have the passion for the journey—not the event—of the higher calling of education; and can love and gift—for themselves as well as others.

The first of the following two stories provides an example of the critical nature of knowing and understanding one's inner core, and its relationship to influencing and leading others, while the second shows how having the "wrong kind" of inner core can lead to false hope and lack of real success.

THE STATESMAN

> If elected, I shall not, either in the matter of appointments to office or assent to legislation, or in shaping any part of policy of my administration, submit to the dictation of any person or persons, special interest, or organization . . . I should deem myself forever disgraced should I in even the slightest degree cooperate in any such system or any such transactions as you describe in your characterization of the "boss" system. I regard myself as pledged to the regeneration of the Democratic Party. [5]

There were three significant influences on the early life of young Woodrow ("Tommy") Wilson: his father, his mother, and his religion. His father, the Reverend Joseph Ruggles Wilson, took particular interest in his son, who at an early age showed a lack of assertiveness and confidence. Often, Tommy would be the object of his father's caustic remarks. Yet at the same time, Reverend Wilson had special affection for his son, and together they developed a relationship based upon love, affection, and learning.

Tommy's mother, Jessie, was soft-spoken, reserved, and solemn. There were two reasons for this: her husband was unquestionably the dominant personality in the home, and she was also extremely devoted to protecting her children—especially Tommy—from the violence and uncertainty of the world that living in the South during the Civil War offered.

Just as important to Wilson's development was his religious faith that he inherited and practiced throughout his life. It was his faith and devotion to the ideology of the Southern Presbyterian Church, including the tenet that public service was a duty and calling and a "good Christian" is responsible to provide participation and services in the life of a civil and moral society.

With such a foundation in place, Woodrow would later become a professor, an author, the president of Princeton University (1902–1910), the governor of New Jersey (1910–1912), and the twenty-eighth president of the United States (1913–1921). Historians credit Wilson's presidency with sweeping and significant changes to the political, economic, and social landscape of the United States. Wilson would also be awarded the Nobel Peace Prize for his leadership in bringing the end of World War I and for forging the plan for a League of Nations. Wilson's career is filled with examples of what his core values were—learned from his parents and church—and how such values would influence him as a person and leader throughout his life.

And while there may be more well-known examples when he was the president of the United States, a most significant illustration of his personal values-based leadership occurred when he became governor of New Jersey. A novice to the New Jersey state political arena, Wilson would have to take on the political machine of James Smith Jr., the most powerful politician in the state at the time.

A shrewd businessman from Newark, Smith also owned two newspapers, had been a member of the Newark Common Council from 1883 to 1887, and was elected to the US Senate, serving from 1893 to 1899. Accordingly, one Tammany Hall leader stated, "Sugar Jim is the greatest one-man politician in the country."

In the spring of 1910, Wilson's path crossed with Smith's. Wilson, who was still the president of Princeton at the time, was approached by a number of influential businessmen and politicians from New Jersey, asking him to consider being the Democratic candidate for the governor of the state. Behind this group was James Smith Jr., who was concerned that a progressive wing of the state Democratic Party was gaining strength in seeking reforms in how Smith and his machine controlled state and local nominating processes. Smith and the machine supported Wilson for the governorship in hope that the university president, with little political experience, could be easily controlled and forever in Smith's debt.

However, to Smith's dismay, Wilson immediately began aligning himself with the progressives toward the end of the convention and then during the campaign as well. On November 8, 1920, Woodrow Wilson won the gubernatorial election in a landslide.

But Smith was not finished. Even though Smith had promised Wilson during the past summer that he would not run for the Senate under any condition, within weeks of the election, James Smith announced that he would, in fact, be a candidate for the US Senate from New Jersey. Wilson did not back down. On December 24, 1910, a headline in the *New York Times* proclaimed,

SMITH BROKE FAITH, WILSON DECLARES.
Promised Not to Run for New Jersey if Doctor Would Try for Governor.

At the very center of this entire episode was Wilson's view of what is fair and just—in life and in politics as well. Everything that Smith stood for went against the inner core of who Woodrow Wilson was. For Wilson, it was his deep sense of order and responsibility that he learned and experienced through his lifelong connection with the doctrines of the Southern Presbyterian Church. Included in these doctrines was the responsibility of leaders to use their authority for the good of the people, and confront those who use their authority to oppress those they are supposed to be serving. His message was clear, focused, and explicit:

Mr. James Smith Jr., represents not a party but a system—a system of political control which does not belong to either party. [6]

One week after his inauguration, the legislature convened in Trenton to select the next senator. Wilson and the progressives had James Martine, a little-known party worker and locally elected official from Union County, to oppose Smith. Wilson referred to the choice between Martine and Smith as a choice between honor and impropriety. In a speech prior to the vote, the governor said to the legislature:

You can turn aside from the measure if you choose; you can decline to follow me . . . but you cannot deprive me of power so long as I steadfastly stand for what I believe to be the interests and legitimate demands of the people themselves. [7]

On January 25, 1910, James Smith Jr. was easily defeated by James Martine. Not only had this election ended the political career of Smith but it also moved Wilson to a place of political prominence—within New Jersey and beyond its borders. And this, after being governor for all of eight days!

Wilson was now able to enact a legislative program, including legislation aimed at ridding the state of the old political machines and corrupt political practices, demonstrating Wilson's dedication and commitment to being a civil authority who is the servant of God and the people—the very foundation of who Woodrow Wilson was.

BIG MIKE'S FIVE COMMANDMENTS

When the maintenance crew showed up at the door of his office, the superintendent was sitting at his desk, staring at the cardboard boxes filled with books, plaques, and framed pictures that had accumulated over the past couple of decades. This was Michael Ryan's last day on the job as the superintendent of schools for Madison City Schools.

Michael had been superintendent for almost three years, until recently, when the board of education informed him that his contract would not be renewed at the end of the current school year. Today was his last day.

Michael told the workers to come in, pointed at the boxes, and said, "Those are the things that need to go. Be careful, some of those things can break." He paused and then stood up, pointing at the chair he had just been sitting in and said, "Don't forget this chair. A gift from Dad. Wrap it and please be careful." While the workers took care of moving Michael's possessions to the waiting truck out back, Michael thinks of his father—"Big Mike" Ryan, the man everyone in Madison City knew.

"Big Mike" Ryan worked for the Department of Public Works for the city. Standing well over six feet tall and weighing more than 250 pounds, he was crew chief for the DPW that cleared the streets of the snow in the winter and maintained the city parks during the other three seasons. Unless there was an unusually big winter storm, Mike and the crew worked the 7:00 a.m. to 3:30 p.m. shift, Monday through Friday.

Ryan was boss of the city workers' union. Being in that position had its perks, including that "Big Mike" would always be on the day shift. This was very important to him since he also owned a bar, aptly called The Irish Still. The bar was located right along Grand Avenue, where three of the biggest factories in Madison City were located. From the late 1930s through the late 1970s, these factories employed thousands of workers, three shifts a day, five days a week. Traditionally, the day shift ended at 4:00 p.m., the afternoon shift at midnight, and then the "graveyard" shift at 8:00 a.m. And every day, before going home, workers would stop in at the bars along Grand Avenue, including The Irish Still. And "Big Mike" was always at the bar when the shifts would change.

Mike's son, Michael, started working at the bar at the age of fifteen, mostly cleaning up, changing the kegs, and sometimes even tending bar when his father had to leave. When Michael turned seventeen, he got a job with the DPW, working on the truck with his father. Michael's high school years were filled with work, sports, and school.

It was during those years working that Michael learned and experienced his father's Five Commandments in real time. "Big Mike" would remind everyone on a regular basis who the boss was and made sure that everyone— at the bar, at the DPW, and at home—understood these commandments:

Commandment 1: Work hard; don't expect any handouts.
Commandment 2: Never trust those in charge, unless you are in charge.
Commandment 3: Use your charm when necessary.
Commandment 4: Bend but don't break the rules.
Commandment 5: Whatever it takes!

Michael became a pretty good athlete in high school and had good grades as well. He attended a state college where he was able to play baseball and graduate with a teaching degree. Of course, during the summers, it was back home to work at his father's bar and for the DPW.

When he finished college, Michael was hired to teach and coach baseball at a little high school about an hour away from Madison City. Within five years, he had established himself as a very good teacher and coach, so it wasn't surprising when he was asked to apply for a teaching and coaching position back in his hometown.

Five years later, once again Michael had used his talents in the classroom and on the athletic field to earn numerous awards and honors. By the age of thirty-two, he became an assistant principal, and by thirty-five, Michael became the principal of his alma mater, Madison City High School. The school showed dramatic improvement under his leadership, and once again, Michael was the recipient of accolades from throughout the community. The Five Commandments were never far from his thoughts and actions.

During the fifth year of being principal, the superintendent of the school district abruptly retired, and the board of education decided to forgo a search by naming Michael Ryan its new superintendent of schools!

As the new superintendent, Michael brought a new enthusiasm to the school district. He visited schools often. He spoke at civic breakfasts, marched in parades, and was always seen at high school sporting events. He created committees to change curriculum, to advise him on teacher evaluations, and to bring about other changes he thought were necessary. He made his father very proud!

But it was late in his second year that things began to unravel for Michael. First, there was an incident with the workers representing noncertified school employees who filed a grievance over the dismissal of a bus driver. The bus driver, who had been with the school district for more than three decades, had spoken out against a new policy Michael had implemented, which had not been approved or even discussed by the board.

During the fall of the next school year, a board member accused Michael of not being forthcoming regarding financial reports that the board had requested on numerous occasions.

Next, a letter from the teachers' union was sent to the board of education, accusing Michael of intimidating nontenured teachers when he was principal of the high school. According to the letter, Michael threatened to not recom-

mend tenure to three teachers unless they made sure students who were in
jeopardy of not graduating on time actually passed the required senior
courses. The students graduated, and the teachers received tenure the next
year.

Then, in February of his third year, Michael informed the board that he
was not recommending tenure for the principal of one of the elementary
schools. This principal was very popular, particularly in the neighborhood
where the school was located. But she, like the bus driver, could be outspok-
en at times, and Michael felt it was in his own best interests to not have this
principal be retained. The board did not support Michael's decision.

Over the next few weeks, there were several special board meetings held
in executive session to discuss this and other issues regarding the superintendent. Sometimes Michael was invited in to the session, and other times, he
was told to stay outside.

At the end of the last executive session, Michael stood up, smiled at the
board, and said, "Well, I'm not changing my mind, I'm not recommending
her for tenure, I'm not apologizing, I haven't done anything wrong." He then
smiled, said "good evening" to everyone, and left the meeting.

LEARNING FOR LEADING

For each of the people presented in this chapter, their inner core was established early in their life and then built upon through various life experiences.
Woodrow Wilson never drifted away from the values that had been instilled
in him at an early age. They were simple, Christian values of honesty, faith,
integrity, and service to others. He knew what these values were; he practiced these values, and he led with these values.

Like Wilson, Michael Ryan had learned a lot about life and success at an
early age, especially from his father. Michael was able to use his inner core
to move up from a successful teacher and coach to principal and finally, to
superintendent. But unlike Wilson, the foundation for Michael's inner core
was more about personal success than the greater good, more about using
others than serving others. And it all came crashing down at the end.

Thus, the lesson for school leaders is twofold. First, to be successful in
this role, one's inner core must be identified, nurtured, practiced, and modeled for others to observe. Second, this inner core needs to be one that is
based upon principles such as integrity, service, and the greater good. Jim
Collins, in his book *From Good to Great*, describes a Level 5 leader as one
who leaves his ego at the door but brings in a passion for the success of the
organization.

How, then, can a school leader (aspiring or current) make sure that she or
he will lead in a manner that is consistent with their own inner core, and at

the same time, serve the greater good of the school, its staff, students, parents, and community? The following are suggested practices:

- *Make a List (and check it more than twice!).* Start by making a list of your core values and beliefs. Share them with loved ones, close friends, and colleagues. Then, post them in prominent places, such as the office, on the desk at home, on the nightstand next to the bed, or even in the car! At the beginning of each day, ask: What will I, as the leader of the school, do today that reflects these values? And at the end of the day, before getting into bed, think about: What did I do today to model such behaviors? Having a calendar nearby can help, in that each time you model a particular core value, you place a plus sign on the calendar for that particular date. Watching the plus signs add up over time can be very motivational and rewarding.
- *Find the Superstars.* Todd Whitaker suggests that there are a small group of superstars in every school. He characterizes these very special teachers as the ones who students want to be in their class; the parents want their children in their class; the rest of faculty respects these teachers for the professionalism and passion they exhibit for teaching; and these teachers represent the best of the best.
- *Develop Relationships with the Superstars.* It is through this group that the school leader can ask the very simple yet defining questions, such as: How am I doing? What's working? Not working? Are my values and beliefs in alignment with the rest of the school? If not, what can I do? This is not easy to do, and this conversation cannot happen the first day, week, or month on the job. But over time, this kind of relationship with the superstars can bring tremendous benefits to your leadership and school success. So who are the superstars where you work? Now, go find them and start talking with them!
- *Take a Hike.* Learning something new is not always linear. Nor is it easy. And time consuming. Yet when it comes to learning new ideas, human nature often sends us in the direction of what we are comfortable with. That may be safe, but it won't likely help us discover or uncover our inner core.

  Going to new places (the world is full of out-of-the-way places), trying new things (take piano lessons at fifty!), or just making sure that you take some time for yourself is important since your life should be defined by you, not what your roles and identities are. And certainly not by what others think you should be. As Dr. Seuss proclaims, "Oh the things you can find if you don't stay behind." And from such experience come the strengthening of your inner core as well.
- *Find a Mentor.* Whether at the district or the school level, school leadership can be daunting at times. So much can be happening all at once—or

at least it seems such—that it is not difficult for the leader to lose sight of the "big picture." Your thoughts may not be crystal clear at times; you may be tending to nonimportant issues that are draining away the ability to lead successfully. We all know that leadership can be a lonely place at times. And most troubling is that you, the leader, may not even know that you have moved away from your inner core—or worse, never even uncovered it.

Having a mentor can provide the school leader with support and guidance, particularly from "outside looking in." This mentor is not someone who is directly associated with the school/school district, but it may be someone with significant leadership experience who is willing to listen, counsel, and encourage the school leader on informal yet regular bases, helping the leader stay grounded with their inner core. There is much research on mentoring, but one aspect of this is critical to leadership success: the leader should not wait until things go bad to find a mentor. It is very important to find a mentor early on in leadership and keep this person close over time.

School leaders will not reach their potential for excellence without having a deep understanding of their inner core—who they are, what they believe in, and how they act on such. To some leaders, this understanding may develop over the course of their life, having learned it from an early age through parental guidance and love, religion, and social experiences.

On the other hand, others may not have had such experiences, and their inner core may have been locked, undiscovered, somewhere deep in their soul. It may take a life-altering event to unlock the core—divorce, being fired, death of a loved one. It might be discovered through other, less stressful means, such as reading, reflection, or friendships.

Once this occurs, the core can become the foundation for leadership action—both personal and professional. And of course, the power of this discovery and the resulting potential in terms of leadership can be amazing to both leader and follower, but most important to the leader.

The most important group one will lead is a rather small group. It is a group of one—you. When the inner core is discovered, practiced, and acted upon, self-leadership will occur. And only then will one be able to lead others. How exhilarating it will be!

Chapter Two

The Magic Behind the Meaning

"I thought Oz was a great Head," said Dorothy.

"And I thought Oz was a lovely Lady," said the Scarecrow.

"And I thought Oz was a terrible Beast," said the Tin Woodman.

"And I thought Oz was a Ball of Fire," exclaimed the Lion.

"No, you are all wrong," said the little man meekly. "I have been making believe."

"Making believe!" cried Dorothy. "Are you not a Great Wizard?"

"Hush, my dear," he said. "Don't speak so loud, or you will be overheard—and I should be ruined. I'm supposed to be a Great Wizard."

"And aren't you?" she asked.

"Not a bit of it, my dear; I'm just a common man." [1]

It was most difficult and disappointing for Dorothy and her friends to learn the "Great Oz" was, in fact, not a wizard who could fulfill their dreams and wishes, but just a regular person, hiding behind a curtain, pretending to be someone that he wasn't. Yet it was also interesting that each of the four travelers had different images in their mind of who and what the "Great Oz" was. To each of them, Oz was a symbol—an object, figure, image, gesture, or character—that represented something important and meaningful.

As "life-long travelers," people experience a myriad of events, actions, and images that encompass and represent life, often in the form of symbols. Symbols can come in the form of logos, phrases, images, pictures, caricatures, and so forth, and we often begin the process of finding meaning of the symbols through our senses, primarily through our eyes, ears, and heart.

A symbol is an object that stands for an idea, image, belief, or action, and it can take the form of words, gestures, visual images, sounds, and other forms of communication. Symbols are found everywhere—in the home, on the street, in schools, churches, in businesses, in the media, in parks, in sports, and so on. And while some symbols can be interpreted by most in a similar manner—for example, the red-yellow-green color pattern of a traffic light—other symbols may take on different meanings to different people. We know that certain gestures done within one culture may seem perfectly acceptable, yet if one were to do the same gesture in another culture, a conflict may likely develop!

Symbols can be very powerful, as they can inspire and unite people to do things that they never thought were possible. They can remind people of the good things in the world as well as the terrible things. Symbols can be a source of hope or one of despair. They can make us laugh, make us cry, make us wonder, help us understand, or help us cope with a world that is sometimes difficult to understand. Symbols can be one of the most effective ways for humans to communicate and connect.

People want to make sense of these experiences, especially when such experiences are extreme in nature. People interpret a particular event. What happened? What did I see? What did I hear? How did I feel? And interestingly, people can interpret the same exact event in many different ways, which is why, for example, the reliability of a witness's testimony in a trial can often be brought into question by lawyers.

Following the 9/11 terrorist attacks on the United States, houses of worship across the nation reported a significant increase in attendance over the next few months. People experienced the event—either from close up or at a distance—made meaning from it, and then decided to act by going to worship and being with other members of the community. Yet at the same time, in other places of the world, there were celebrations of the successful attacks. Once again, these particular people experienced the event, interpreted it, and then acted, again often in groups. And finally, there probably were people in the world who experienced this event, interpreted it as "oh well," and took action by doing nothing.

School districts and schools, as organizations, are encompassed as well with events that take place in which the "players" (students, teachers, administrators, staff, parents, and the community) experience an event, interpret and make meaning of it, and then respond in a particular way. And as often happens, the same event can lead to different interpretations and responses.

Take, for example, the following event that may occur in a school. As you read each of the scenarios from this event, think of your interpretations and reactions and others' interpretations and reactions.

- The principal of the high school sits down in her office to quickly eat lunch, when the secretary walks in and says, "There is a fight in the cafeteria." The principal immediately leaves the office and quickly makes her way to the cafeteria.
- Along the way, a teacher says to the principal, "It's a fight between two boys."
- As the principal arrives at the cafeteria, she notices one of the boys fighting is white and the other is black.

The principal, along with several other teachers, manage to stop the fight and bring the two students to the office for disciplinary action. However, the following comments are made by some of the "players" in the school:

- Student A: "That was really cool, tomorrow it's my turn!"
- Teacher A: "Those two are always in trouble, but the boss won't do anything all to them. If it happens near me, I'm looking the other way."
- Student B: "I don't feel safe in the cafeteria anymore. I'll eat my lunch in the library or go without . . . but I'm not going back to the cafeteria anymore."
- Teacher B: "I think we have racial issues in this school, and tomorrow, I am going to meet with the principal to try to come up with some ideas to improve the culture here."
- Student C: "What's the big deal . . . it happens all the time. I just go about my business."
- Teacher C: "I'm going to our union rep about this!"

In addition, by the end of the day the local newspaper calls to inquire about "all the fights" taking place at the school and wants to know if they are racially motivated or not. The superintendent's office has left a message for the principal to call his office as soon as possible, and the parents of both students involved in the fight are in the main office, demanding to see the principal.

This single event now has multiple meanings and reactions. In addition, many of those connected to the school—either directly or indirectly—will now begin to have images of what is occurring in the school, and subsequently take action. If, for instance, people at the school do not feel safe, the principal may request additional security officers for the school. If this occurs, how will the "players" interpret this and then react? Will some of the "players" grasp onto the traditional symbols, images, or phrases of the school as a source of comfort and guidance? Will others begin to create new symbols and images in response to this new reality?

This chapter focuses on the symbolic nature of leadership and the symbolic roles school leaders play in carrying out their duties, roles, and responsibilities. Inherent in this discussion is the idea that the followers of the leader may have a unique perception and image of what a leader should do and how to behave. And just as Dorothy and her friends had different images, so do followers. Individuals may have totally different images and expectations in their mind of the leader. Subsequently, as the leader acts, followers interpret these actions, make decisions, and then act upon such. These interpretations, decisions, and actions of the followers may or may not be similar, which can impact the leader's future actions. And then the process begins to repeat itself.

Just as followers may differ on their perceptions and images of leadership, so may leaders. Obviously, the role of a school superintendent is to lead the school district, and the role of a principal is to lead a school. As the superintendent acts, how aware is she of the messages she is sending and how they are being interpreted? Furthermore, are there specific actions that the superintendent can take to "send a message" in an explicit or implicit manner? And how can a school leader become cognizant of the critical nature that symbolic leadership can have on her success in leading the district to higher levels of success?

Consider what a college professor does with graduate students during their first-ever school leadership class:

> The professor begins by asking students to write down the names of the five greatest leaders they have ever encountered—historically, during their life, or even personally. Once the students make their list, the professor asks them to write a brief description of why they chose these particular leaders. Students generally included names such as Abraham Lincoln, Martin Luther King Jr., Mohandas Gandhi, Jesus Christ, among others.
>
> Students are also asked to make a list of, in their opinion, the worst leaders. Usually, the list includes tyrants and dictators, unscrupulous politicians, and just plain "bad" people who happened to be in leadership roles.
>
> In addition to historical figures, sometimes students include contemporary leaders from business (CEOs) to sports (coaches and players) to personal experiences (parent, current principal, pastor, etc.), and even some contemporary pop culture figures! The discussion will then focus on why these people were listed, what similarities and differences there were, and then to the eventual development of a working definition of leader and leadership.
>
> But what the professor finds as the most interesting and enlightening is when students are given a generic list of animals and other living species, and then are asked to select one that best represents, in their opinion, their overall perception of the image of leaders and leadership (the good and/or the bad). Once selected, each student draws a representation of the species onto a piece of newsprint. The drawings are placed on the walls of the classroom, and the students, along with the professor, engage in a gallery walk.
>
> Over time, some of the more popular images include a lion, fox, shark, eagle, angel, dove, gazelle, and chameleon, to name a few. Of course, for

students with a less-than-positive image of leaders and leaderships, examples
have included images of a snake, a pit bull, the devil, and a charging bull!

According to the professor, a critical component of this activity is not
only to have students begin the process of reflecting on who leaders are and
what leadership is but also what these two symbolize to them: what is their
own interpretation and what deeper meanings such thoughts engender. And
from this inquiry, a framework begins to evolve regarding the relationship of
leaders and leadership to symbols and symbolism.

SYMBOLIC ROLES OF EXEMPLARY SCHOOL LEADERS: FROM THE OUTSIDE LOOKING IN

Two perspectives on the relationship between leadership and symbolism are
now presented. The first will be from the "outside looking in"—how followers and others perceive leadership in terms of what leaders "should look like"
and how a leader "should act," and the meanings of such perceptions.

For example, in the early nineteenth century, scholars in the field of
leadership provided much evidence to support the thesis that great leaders
"are made, not born," and that leadership is not something that is learned. To
these scholars, this Great Man Theory was thought of in terms of traits that
were male dominated, and associated with physical factors (e.g., strength,
height, facial features), personality features (e.g., extrovert, dominator, pater-
nalistic), and ability (decision maker, problem solver, effective communica-
tor). To some, both birthright and divine intervention became a foundation
for such "natural" leaders to emerge.

Over the past half-century or more, much of the Great Man Theory has
been dismissed and replaced by terms of traits that are "more of nurture and
less of nature," and that such qualities as honesty, persistence, self-confi-
dence, integrity, and intelligence can not only be defined but can also be
learned and then applied.

Yet it is worth noting that the Great Man Theory, particularly in the
United States, is still evident within the culture and context of leadership.
And while some may contend that our society is evolving away from this
construct, others suggest that all one needs to do is look at leadership through
two particular lenses—gender and ethnicity—to see that it is not evolving at
a pace that is representative of the demographics of society. And if this in
fact is true, then when followers and others think of who a typical leader
should be, perhaps many are still thinking along the lines of traditional features of gender, ethnicity, physique, and personality as what the leader
should "look like," and ultimately, they make decisions based upon that.

In the field of education, there is data that strongly suggests that the Great
Man Theory still dominates leadership, not only in the numbers of leaders

who represent what this theory posits but also how followers and others may perceive who, in fact, should be a school leader. According to the National Center for Education Statistics, more than 76 percent of the teachers in public schools across America are females, yet only slightly more than 50 percent of the principals are female, including only 30 percent of high school principals.[2] In terms of ethnicity, more than 82 percent of the principals are white, yet more than 47 percent of students across the country attending public schools are nonwhite.[3]

The data from the context of the school superintendency is not much more encouraging. According to the American Association of School Administrators (2011), less than 25 percent of the superintendents are females, and less than 5 percent are nonwhite. Neither of these figures is close to representing either the demographics of teachers or students. Perhaps the glass ceilings and glass walls that are often the result of people's images of what a school leader "should look like" are more prevalent than expected.

SYMBOLIC ROLES OF EXEMPLARY SCHOOL LEADERS: FROM THE INSIDE LOOKING OUT

Being able to communicate is always near the top of the list of traits associated with effective leadership. As mentioned earlier, people want to make meaning of what is occurring around them every day. When tragic events within an organization or a community take place, people will look to leaders for answers. When people are faced with significant change, they will often look to leaders for guidance and support. Effective leaders can use a multitude of ways to provide support in these instances, no more powerful but easily misunderstood than communicating through symbols and symbolism. Three such frameworks are now presented.

In their book, *The Wizard and the Warrior: Leading with Passion and Power* (2006), Bolman and Deal present leadership in four distinct yet interrelated frames: analysts (rationale, logic, facts), caregivers (people, feelings, and relationships), warriors (conflict, politics, and scarce resources), and wizards (imagination, meaning, and insight). They submit that most leaders gravitate toward the analysts and caregivers because of traditional means by which people learn to lead, and because many are afraid of the political nature of leadership and do not understand the wizardry of leadership—as if it is unseemly, lacking in foundation, perhaps even fraudulent.

However, in their research, Bolman and Deal contend that effective leaders are those who embrace the warrior and the wizard by learning and understanding the essentials of how such can enhance leadership and success. They suggest:

Our goal is to revive the positive aspects of magic and wizardry, and to link them to the challenges a leader faces today. How does a leader create or transform an organization, relying heavily on symbols to produce both tangible and mystical results that capture imagination and loyalty? How can a leader avoid the traps and resist the darker side of magic, which produces destruction instead of positive creation or transformation?[4]

In their work, the authors present both the good and the bad side of the leaders as a wizard: "authentic wizard," "wannabe wizard," and "harmful wizard." They do submit, however, that consistent among these three types of wizards is the effective use by the leader of myths, rituals, ceremonies, stories, images, icons, values, and even "body language." For each of these, it requires a skilled leader to align the message of her actions to such symbols in a way that will motivate followers, pique the interest and imagination of followers, create a heartfelt response, or have the followers thinking in a manner that they had not previously experienced.

Edgar Schein (2010) proposed that there are a number of tools that a leader can use to influence how people within the organization "perceive, think, feel, and behave based upon their own [the leader's] conscious and unconscious convictions."[5] While Schein considers each to be visible, each also provides a context to which the followers interpret and make meaning of the action, and then act accordingly. Schein refers to these as "Primary Embedding Mechanisms," as presented with examples from a school context.

- *What leaders pay attention to, measure, and control on a regular basis*: If a school principal informs everyone that instructional time during the school day is of paramount importance, how often does he interrupt classes with announcements over the public address system?
- *How leaders react to critical incidents and organization crises*: A superintendent announces the closing of a school, which has been part of the district for almost a century. The parents and community are stunned. To what extent does the superintendent, through her actions and words, provide support for this grieving community?
- *How leaders allocate resources*: To what extent does the budget that the superintendent proposes to the board of education align to the beliefs, mission, and vision of the school district?
- *How leaders model, teach, and coach*: To what extent does the principal model effective teaching methods during weekly faculty meetings?
- *How leaders reward and sanction*: How does a principal discipline two teachers for a similar offense, with one teacher popular among students and staff, while the other is not well thought of by students and staff?
- *How leaders recruit, select, promote, and excommunicate*:[6]

In each of the examples listed, the action of the school leader will obviously be important, but of equal value will be how followers and others find meaning. If the leader, for example, is inconsistent or even fails to act, people will take meaning from this, which will then become part of the culture of the school/school district—"that's the way we do things around here." On the other hand, the leader that is very deliberate and thoughtful about words and actions as they pertain to the six mechanisms that Schein proposes will have a much better opportunity to manage the message, and not leave such to an uniformed or unrefined interpretation.

School leaders play a very pivotal role in the development and sustainability of the school culture. Such a culture can have an impact on how people—teachers, students, and parents—think, perceive, act, and feel about the school. Just as in any organization, a culture will emerge within a school, and a wise and savvy leader will want to play a major role in its development, particularly with the use of symbols and symbolism.

Deal and Peterson (2009) submit that "one of the most significant roles of leaders is the creation, encouragement and refinement of the symbols and symbolic activity that confer meaning."[7] In fact, they contend that a school leader can (and should) play a significant role in shaping and sustaining a strong culture. Deal and Peterson suggest that the leader can play the following symbolic roles in support of the mission and vision of the school:

- *Historian*: seeks to understand and appreciate the social and normative past of the school.
- *Sleuth*: analyzes and probes for the current array of cultural traditions, values, and beliefs.
- *Visionary*: works with others to characterize a portrait of the ideal school.
- *Icon*: affirms values through dress, behavior, attention, actions, and routines.
- *Potter*: shapes and is shaped by the school's webbing of heroes, rituals, traditions, ceremonies, and symbols.
- *Poet*: uses expressive language to reinforce values and sustains the school's best image of itself.
- *Actor*: improvises in the school's predictable dramas, comedies, and tragedies.
- *Healer*: oversees transitions and changes; heals the wounds of conflict and loss.[8]

In each of these roles, there is a very strong symbolic presence for the leader to recognize and act upon. In fact, as a school leader takes action in one or more of these roles, again, she is sending a very strong message of what her beliefs are, what she is passionate about, and how these are aligned to the goals of the school. And by being consistent and explicit with such actions, a very strong message will be sent to staff, students, and parents, who in turn will interpret the message and act upon such.

To ignore the critical nature of these roles can be most dangerous, since at some point, *someone* will assume these roles, and it might be someone who, for whatever reasons, may help to build a school culture that is not in the best interests of students, staff, and the community.

THE FEZ AND THE HAT

The form of government may be summarized in a single word: Republic . . . Within a short period of time the form which Turkey has now actually assumed will be confirmed by law. . . . Just as basically, there is no difference between all the Republic of Europe and America . . . so also Turkey's difference from these Republics will be merely a matter of form.
—Mustafa Kemal, 1923

In 1923, the Republic of Turkey was born and its first president was Mustafa Kemal. He had been a military officer during World War I, and when the Allies defeated the Ottoman Empire, Kemal directed the Turkish National Movement during the Turkish War of Independence. Having instituted a temporary government in the city of Ankara, Kemal and the Turkish forces were able to defeat the Allies. As its first president, Kemal would commence a program of reforms in Turkey, aimed at moving the new country into becoming a modern and secular state.

This would certainly not be an easy task, since Turkey was still deeply entrenched in political, economic, and cultural traditions, dating back centuries.

Kemal, who would later be given the title of "Ataturk" (Father of Turkey), knew that if Turkey were to become a state in which it could compare itself with the nations of Europe and America, symbols and images would need to change.

Within the Islamic religion, clothing has a deep symbolic meaning. In Turkey, the acceptable head covering for men was the fez, which had been introduced in the early nineteenth century. Ironically, the fez was manufactured for the Ottoman Empire in Austria. The fez was a simple but very visible symbol of past traditions that Kemal felt needed to change if Turkey was to become a modern state.

Shortly after becoming president, Mustafa Kemal would take a trip to a number of outlying provinces situated between Ankara in central Turkey and the Black Sea in the north. On the surface, it appeared that the purpose of this trip was for the new president to meet and connect with the people and officials of this region. For those living there, all had heard of Mustafa Kemal, but only a few had ever seen him in person.

But there was another reason for this trip. The people in this region were still clinging to the traditional aspects of their culture, and Kemal wanted to surprise and stun the people with the introduction of a more Western and modern way for men to dress.

He left Ankara bareheaded in an open car. Everywhere on the journey, throngs of people greeted Kemal as their national hero. Throughout the towns and villages, portraits of Kemal had been painted on buildings, and town squares were decorated and festivities were organized in anticipation of his arrival. Some of the towns even covered their main street with a red carpet for him to walk on upon arrival.

When Kemal and his cortege would arrive at the outskirts of a town, Kemal would usually get out of the car and begin to walk down the street, greeting the people on both sides. And most times, he was met with polite silence. Kemal was clean shaven, wore a European-style suit with an open-neck shirt, and on his head was a white Panama hat.

Most Turks were shocked. Had this occurred a decade earlier, Kemal may have been beaten or stoned by the crowd—but not today! The president was presenting an image that people were not accustomed to, yet he would continue. In each town, he spoke to the people, praising them for their hard work, dedication, and sacrifices in support of their independence. He danced traditional dances with the people, sang traditional songs, and sat among the people to eat with them as well. And in every instance, he was either wearing his Panama hat or carrying it in his hand.

Toward the end of the trip, Kemal arrived at Inebolu, a small port on the Black Sea. Speaking to an audience that was mostly dressed in traditional clothing, Kemal stated:

> Internationally accepted civilized dress suits us too. Shoes or boot on your feet, trousers on your legs, then shirt, collar and tie, waistcoat, jacket and, to complete it all, headgear with a sun-shield, which I want to call by its proper name: it's called a hat.
>
> We will become civilized . . . we will march forward . . . for civilization is a fearful fire which consumes those who ignore it. [9]

As Mustafa Kemal made his way back to Ankara, news agencies across Turkey reported what he had both said *and* what he had worn. Upon arrival, family, friends, and officials greeted him, all wearing hats. And it wasn't long until hats and Western suits became the norm for fashion for officials and members of the professional class, eventually to include the rest of Turkey as well.

Later that year, a law was enacted by the assembly that made the wearing of a fez a criminal offense, and the law also required *all* men to wear hats. Initially, there were not enough hats for the men of Turkey to wear, so hats were imported from throughout Europe. However, within several years, the

Turkish hat industry had come into existence and became a vibrant part of
the new economy.

While simple yet daring, Kemal's strategy was taking a simple piece of
clothing—the fez—and making it a symbol of an era from which Turkey was
moving, and replacing it with the more modern hat found in Europe and
America. The meaning was clear: Turkey was moving ahead, and more significant as well, reforms were on the way.

CHARKHA AND KHADI

> I am convinced that swaraj [self-rule] cannot come so long as the tens of
> millions of our brothers and sisters do not take to the charkha [spinning wheel]
> do not spin, do not make khadi [homespun cloth] and wear it.
> —Mohandas Gandhi, 1924 [10]

It was in 1920 when Mohandas Gandhi decided to initiate a movement of
noncooperation against the British ruling system that had dominated India for
centuries. Frustrated by the lack of willingness by the British to allow India
to self-govern in any form, Gandhi's strategy was not only aimed at the
British but inwardly as well. As he stated, "The English have not taken India,
we have given it to them. They are not in India because of their strength, but
because we allow them." [11]

One of the many crippling effects of British rule in India was caused by
the East India Company, which had been chartered in the late seventeenth
century to enhance trade between the British Empire and the Far East, including the Indian subcontinent. Although dissolved in 1874, many of the trade
and manufacturing policies were continued through the support of the British
government and its representatives in India.

Of particular distaste to Gandhi and other Indians was the British policy
of forcing Indians to wear clothing that was manufactured in England and
then transported to India for the people to purchase. According to Gandhi,
the foreign cloth represented "the blood, the death, the slavery of Indians"
imposed by the British.

On July 31, 1921, tens of thousands of Indians had gathered in Bombay to
hear Gandhi speak. In his speech, he alluded to the symbolism of Indians
wearing clothes that were made in the textile plants of England and then
forced upon the Indians to wear. Gandhi called for the destruction of all
foreign clothes as a symbol of Indian self-respect and self-determination.

During this and subsequent speeches, Gandhi called for the rebirth of the
Indian domestic cloth industry. At the heart of this, according to Gandhi, was
that Indians would now forsake any and all foreign clothing, and replace such
with khadi, the homespun woven cloth made by the Indians themselves.
Indians, said Gandhi, would spin their own clothing, using the charkha,

which had once been the symbol of the Indian textile industry. Gandhi would later state,

> The charkha represents to me the hope of the masses. The masses lost their freedom, such as it was, with the loss of the charkha. The charkha supplemented the agriculture of the villagers and gave it dignity. It was the friend and solace of the widow. It kept the villagers from idleness. For the charkha included all the anterior and posterior industries—ginning, carding, warping, sizing, dyeing and weaving. These in turn kept the village carpenter and blacksmith busy. The charkha enabled the seven hundred thousand villages to become self-contained. With the exit of the charkha went the other village's industries.
>
> Nothing took the place of these industries. Therefore the villagers were drained of their varied occupations and their creative talent and what little wealth these brought them. Hence, if the villagers are to come into their own, the most natural thing that suggests itself is the revival of the charkha and all it means.[12]

Toward the end of the speech in Bombay, Gandhi, wearing khadi (homespun clothing), lit a bonfire of collected foreign clothing in hope that "flames would go so high that they would be seen all the way to the textile mills of Birmingham and Leeds." Thousands of others joined with Gandhi that evening. He hoped that the fire would not die out, and that similar fires would be lit "every day, every week, in every town and street of India."

As the bonfires swept across India, so did khadi. Indians began wearing the homespun clothing as both a sign of self-respect and defiance of British rule. In villages and towns, the charkha was brought back to prominence as Indians began to make and wear their own clothes. Everywhere Gandhi went, he would bring his spinning wheel, often weaving his own cloth while giving speeches to friends and foes alike. Other times, when surrounded by dozens of followers, Gandhi would go off by himself to spin. And more often than not, others would do the same.

The interpretation of this action was significant and meaningful—the slow and sometimes painful movement toward swaraj. The success of the bonfires, the return of the spinning wheels, and the subsequent wearing of the homespun cloth provided a symbol of hope for India in its quest for freedom. It became the foundation for future actions taken by Gandhi and the people of India against the British and the imperialistic policies.

This action also became symbolic as the people of India could begin to be proud of who they were and what they could accomplish, even if the odds were decidedly against them. It also began to shift the Indian people away from self-pity and hopelessness to what Gandhi would refer to as "the creation of utter disgust with ourselves that we have thoughtlessly decked ourselves at the expense of the poor—ourselves."

This noncooperation began to arouse the people of India in a manner never seen before. From villages to the cities, mill workers, peasants, small shop owners, and street people alike began to volunteer and participate in this movement.

The meaning of this movement would be the first of many alarms for the British government in which to respond. It was one thing if the subjects of the Empire were to take up arms in protest. This could be easily quashed with the might of the British navy and army. But the subjects were not taking up arms. They were practicing civil disobedience. And if the numbers of those participating were limited, then there were plenty of jails for them in which to be placed.

But this was not the case. The number of participants was in the tens of millions and being led by one person—Mohandas Gandhi—with his charkha and khadi. As Winston Churchill would later say—and many within England would assent to—

> It is alarming and also nauseating to see Mr. Gandhi, a seditious Middle Temple lawyer now posing as a fakir of a type well-known in the East, striding half-naked up the steps of the Vice-regal palace, while he is organizing and conducting a campaign of civil disobedience, to parley on equal terms with the representative of the King-Emperor. Such a spectacle can only increase the unrest in India and the danger to which white people there are exposed. [13]

This is exactly the image and message Gandhi wanted to send.

HIGH FIVES

Armand "Armie" Rizzo had always been a "people person." In high school, he was president of the student council for *three* straight years, was voted most popular and most likely to succeed by his fellow classmates, and always seemed to be in the middle of the excitement that was prevalent during this time of his life. An average athlete, he lettered in three sports during his four years of high school.

Much of this was repeated as Armie went on to a state university where he became an education major with a history minor. He lettered in soccer all four years, was elected to several campuswide student organizations, and again, was voted most popular for his senior class.

There were several reasons why Armie was so popular and well liked. First, he truly liked being around people. He learned this from his father, who owned a clothing store in a local shopping center. His father would meet and greet every customer with enthusiasm, a big smile, and either a firm hand-shake, pat on the back, or a hug. And his father knew how to listen to people as well—making eye contact throughout the entire conversation, head nodding slightly up and down. Armie learned this well.

Armie also has a wonderful smile. Friends would often reminisce about never seeing a frown on Armie's face, even when things were going bad (like the time in high school when their basketball team lost fifteen games in a row!). This smile, though, was a symbol of his love for life and the enthusiasm he put into every day. And fellow students and teachers, whether in high school or college, naturally gravitated toward Armie.

Naturally, when he became a teacher, Armie brought his enthusiasm and love for live, along with his smile, with him. Over time, he developed a positive rapport with students, as his lessons were known to be creative and full of surprises on a regular basis (wearing masks and costumes, for example). The only concern that some had was that there seemed to be more style than substance, and Armie's principal encouraged him to balance his lessons with more content. Of course, Armie took this with a smile, and with typical enthusiasm, began taking graduate courses in history.

Armie's signature interaction with students and staff was the "high five." Whether he was standing at his classroom door, walking down the hallway, or even standing in line in the cafeteria, Armie would extend his arm and "high five" the closest people.

Sometimes, he would even walk down the hall and "high five" imaginary people. In the beginning, some students and faculty—especially the older faculty—wondered if this was real or "a show." But over time, most would eventually realize that this "high-fiving," passionate person was, in fact, the "real deal."

Within a decade, Armie had moved into administration, becoming an assistant principal at the school. He brought his enthusiasm and passion to this position as well. Even when dealing with the issues involving students, teachers, and parents, Armie's personality would often go a long way in defusing potential controversies. And particularly with students, every session would end with a "high five."

It was early June, with the end of the school year in sight. Armie had just turned thirty-three and was looking forward to the school's upcoming graduation, and of course, the two weeks with his family at the cottage on the lake. On this particular Tuesday, Armie received a call from the secretary of the school district superintendent, requesting that Armie come to his office at the end of school that day. So at close of school, Armie drove the five miles to the district office to meet with the superintendent. After some small talk, the superintendent shared the following with Armie:

> Armie, you have been at your school now for eleven years, and you have done a terrific job as a teacher and now assistant principal. Your enthusiasm and ability to work with everyone—and I mean everyone—has not gone unno-

ticed. Students, parents, and colleagues always mention to me about what an asset you are to the school.

As you probably are aware, things have not been going well at Western Hills High School. They've had three principals in five years, and now we are looking for another. The students aren't achieving at levels that we want; the culture at the school is toxic, to say the least; and we are beginning to get a lot of pushback from parents, threatening to pull their kids out and send them to private schools or even start a charter school.

We need someone who can turn Western Hills around—someone with experience but someone who can bring people together—the students, the faculty, and the parents—so that everyone can feel positive and good about that school. And I think that person is you. So I am offering you the position of principal at Western Hills, with the main goal in the beginning to rid the school of its toxic culture. Please go home and think about this.

Call me tomorrow and I am hoping that you accept. If you do, you will start on July 1.

Armie accepted the position and negotiated, and after an abbreviated vacation, he started his position as principal of Western Hills High School on July 1. With his natural exuberance, Armie used the summer to meet everyone possible that was connected with the school. Every day, he would give a list to his secretary of people to call, requesting that they come to Armie's office to have "coffee/sodas and conversation." Teachers were called, parents were called, and even students were called to come in. Community leaders were asked to come by. In each meeting, he would focus on three questions: What's working well here at Western Hills? What isn't working well? What do you need from me as your new principal?

By the end of the summer, Armie had met with more than one hundred people. Some of the meetings were one on one, some were small groups, and there were several occasions that groups of eight to ten people would meet with Armie. For each meeting, he focused the conversation around three questions: What's working well here at Western Hills? What isn't working well here? What do you *need* from me, the new principal, to make this school successful?

At the same time, Armie reviewed the history of the school, the people who had been influential throughout its existence, as well as the stories and events that helped shape the current context of Western Hills. By the end of the summer, Armie had confirmed what the superintendent had said about the "toxic culture"; as a matter of fact, the culture was worse than what he had expected. Among the items he found was:

- There existed serious factions among the faculty.
- Students did not trust teachers and felt school was mostly boring and a chore.

- Parents felt they were never listened to and that communication between them and teachers was almost nonexistent.
- The once proud connection between the school and community had been lost and there did not seem to be much interest in having it reenergized.
- Issues related to student grading and discipline, as well as evaluating teacher performance, were inconsistent and applied mostly on an individual basis, which often led to complaints of favoritism, preferential treatment, or unreasonableness.

Armie knew that before he could get people to change *what* they did in the course of the school day, he would have to get them to address *how* they do things. And so, at his first meeting with the faculty in August, and with the first assembly with the students on the first day of school, Armie gave a lesson on how to "high five" to everyone. He begin with a slide show that depicted the evolution in sports of the handshake from "gimme five" to the "high five." Armie then demonstrated the "proper" technique of giving and receiving the "high five."

Next, at a faculty meeting, he asked all staff to stand and practice this with at least five other people in the room. And he did the same in the auditorium with the students. In both cases, he let everyone know that this was how he would greet people and how it would be great if everyone else would as well.

Faculty and students, as a whole, were rather skeptical of this. But he wasnMMMt deterred or discouraged. Everywhere he went, Armie would "high five" with people. And eventually, this began to occur among the students and some of the faculty. But each day, it seemed that more and more "high fives" were being given.

The key, though, to Armie was that the "high five" was a symbol of how people were going to treat each other at Western Hills High School: a smile, a hello, and of course, the "high five." And for Armie, it didn't matter who he was greeting, whether it was the superintendent visiting the school, an upset parent, or students hanging out after school, he would always be modeling the "high five." And as this became part of the culture of the school over time, it was much easier to engage people in addressing issues of student achievement, discipline, teaching and learning, relationships, and morale.

Of course, there were some who were opposed to Armie's style, particularly some of the more veteran teachers. As one teacher stated, "Armie is turning this high school into a 'touchy-feel-good nursery school.' Once you get past the mask of this showman, there's nothing there." Yet the students and their parents, as well as more than a few of the teachers, were becoming much more positive about their experiences at Western Hills.

Over the next couple of years, Armie managed to have student clubs revived, brought in a new athletic director, changed how faculty would become department chairs, and convened a parent-teacher-student association that met for breakfast on a monthly basis. It was from this particular group that a yearlong collaborative process of creating a new set of core values, a mission statement, and a vision statement was started.

Once completed, Armie had faculty members sign the document (just like the signers of the Declaration of Independence!); it was framed and placed in a prominent place for all to see. In addition, copies were placed in every classroom and on the school stationery, and Armie never failed to mention it whenever he spoke to faculty, parents, students, and the community. Often, he would start a conversation or speech by saying, "You know, our mission at Western Hills is to [ ] and so in that spirit, I'd like to discuss the following with you."

Armie also wanted to recognize those teachers who were great in the classroom and exemplified the values, beliefs, and mission of the school. Armie felt that the teachers had the most impact on student learning during the school day, and if they could be more excited, enthusiastic, and supportive toward the students and their colleagues, it would make a huge difference over the long journey.

For example, he had students nominate faculty members for a "teacher-of-the-month" recognition. On the first Monday of the month, via the school's television station, the teacher-of-the-month would be announced and interviewed. This teacher would receive a plaque and free lunch on "pizza Friday" for the month. And of course, the interview ended with a "high five" from Armie with the teacher, visible on each of the classroom televisions.

From this group of teachers who had been recognized on a monthly basis, a committee of students, parents, and selected members of the faculty and administration would select the "Western Hills 'Teacher of the Year,'" which would be announced at the end-of-the-year awards assembly. The teacher's picture and a plaque would be hung in the new "Wall of Fame" in the main corridor of the school. In addition, the teacher would receive a preferred parking spot for the year, $1,000 gift from the PTA, and numerous gift cards from local businesses.

Armie was also able to "convince" a local home and garden center to donate a tree for this occasion. After the assembly, faculty and students would go out to the front of the school where a tree would be planted in honor of the recipient. Within a couple of years, any teacher who retired from Western Hills with more than fifteen years at the school also would receive a tree planted in their honor.

In spite of the original skeptics and naysayers, the culture and climate had turned around at Western Hills. It took almost five years, but the image of the school had changed from a place where no one wanted to be to a great place to be a part of. Student achievement had improved, discipline issues had decreased, and teachers who needed to leave had left and were replaced by teachers who really bought into this culture. And of course, the "high five" was an infused, almost second nature of how people greeted and interacted with one another. In addition, the trees in the front of the school began to grow.

It was a Saturday morning in late January when the superintendent received the call. It was from Armie Rizzo's wife, Ella. Late on the previous evening, Armie went to bed around eleven o'clock. When Ella joined him in bed, she discovered he wasn't breathing. Upon arrival to the hospital, Armie was declared dead, from what doctors said was a massive heart attack. The superintendent was stunned, as was the entire Western Hills community as the word spread throughout the weekend.

As expected, Western Hills High School was full of shock, grief, and sorrow on Monday, as both faculty and students tried to make sense of the death of their principal. Armie was in the final months of his sixth year as principal of the school.

The lines to pay respects to Armie Rizzo on Tuesday at the funeral home stretched for blocks without stop from noon until past nine o'clock. The funeral was held on Wednesday. In addition to the family, the superintendent spoke, as did representatives of the faculty and student body.

When the family and friends arrived for the burial at the cemetery, they found two lines of students and faculty awaiting the procession. As the casket was wheeled between the two lines, students and faculty gave each other a solemn and teary-eyed "high five."

And on the first Monday of April, when the ground in front of Western Hills High School was no longer frozen, at the time when the teacher-of-the-month recognition was to normally occur, the entire faculty and staff of Western Hills High School met in the foyer of the high school auditorium, where a sculpture of a "high five," created by a graduate of the high school, was placed on a pedestal.

LEARNING FOR LEADING

Few in the world of leadership—including school leadership—would argue with the critical nature that a school leader plays in exemplifying what a school stands for. As the leader, the superintendent, for example, becomes the face of the school district and its primary advocate, both internally and externally. The same goes for a school principal.

One only has to observe when something exceptional happens to a school district or school—either positive or negative—and the first person usually to speak is the superintendent for the district or the principal of the school. And the meaning from whatever the school leader says or does can be interpreted in terms of answers to questions such as: Who's in charge? Is this person competent? How trustworthy? What is the meaning behind the message?

Most likely, people will draw their own conclusions and act accordingly, particularly if there is an image that portrays the absence of leadership in areas such as technical skills, human relations, and the "big picture." As someone once said, "Is anyone in charge? Does anyone care?"

Thus, school leadership becomes critical in the symbolic context. Since symbolism includes images and their interpretations, everything the school leader says or does provides a view of the portrait of this leader. Subsequently, the only choice the leader has is to either create this portrait in a measured, explicit manner or have the portrait created by chance. The savvy school leader will most likely embrace the former and avoid the latter.

Consider how Lawrence Miller (1984) used symbolism to describe the unrealistic ideal of what leadership is often interpreted as:

> Problems are always solved in the same way. The Lone Ranger and his faithful Indian companion . . . come riding into town. The Lone Ranger, with his mask and mysterious identity, background, and lifestyle, never becomes intimate with those whom he will help. His power is partly in his mystique. Within ten minutes the Lone Ranger has understood the problem, identified who the bad guys are, and has set out to catch them. He quickly outwits the bad guys, draws his gun, and has them behind bars.
>
> And then there was always that wonderful scene at the end [where] the helpless victims are standing in front of their ranch or in the town square marveling at how wonderful it is now that they have been saved, you hear hoof beats, then the "William Tell Overture," and one person turns to another and asks "But who was that masked man?" And another replies, "Why, that was the Lone Ranger!" We see Silver rear up and with hearty "Hi ho, Silver," the Lone Ranger and his companion ride away.
>
> It was wonderful. Truth, justice, and the American Way protected once again.
>
> What did we learn from this cultural hero? Among the lessons that are now acted out daily by managers [leaders] are the following:
>
> • There is always a problem down on the ranch [the school district or school] and someone is responsible.
> • Those who get themselves into the difficulty are incapable of getting themselves out of it. "I'll have to go down," says the leader, "or send someone down to fix it."
> • In order to have the mystical powers needed to solve problems, the leader must stay behind the mask. Don't let the ordinary folks get too close to you or your powers may be lost.
> • Problems need to be solved within discrete periods of time units, and the expectation is they will be solved decisively.

These myths are no laughing matter. Anyone who has lived within or close
to organizations [school districts or schools] knows that these myths are powerful forces in daily life. Unfortunately, none of them bears much resemblance
to the real world. [14]

Thus, the school leader may feel it is critical to lead in this fashion, so that
followers and others feel strongly that "someone is in charge and making
decisions." This, then, perpetuates a dependence upon the leader to have all
of the answers for every situation. Yet what happens if the leader does not
have *the* answer at the particular time others expect it? In addition, such
dependence upon the leader to make all important decisions can create an
environment that enables followers and others to not wish to become part of
the decision-making or problem-solving process, since the Lone Ranger will
do this for them.

All school leaders use symbolic leadership, either purposely or uninten-
tionally. They constantly send messages to followers by what they say, how
they act, and how they make decisions, and as such, followers will take
meaning as to what is and what is not important to the leader. While some
may posit that such symbolic leadership only occurs during extraordinary
times, in fact, it occurs daily with the hundreds of exchanges that take place
not only between the school leader and followers but also subsequently
among the followers as they try to make meaning of the exchange that took
place.

Reflect upon the following exchange between a school principal and a
teacher in her office:

Principal: So, after three formal observations, I still see very little use of
technology in your classes. You know, we spend thousands of dollars from a
grant to get whiteboards in every classroom, and you seem to be one of the
few not using it effectively.

Teacher: Well, I don't use it because I am not yet comfortable with the
whiteboard. A number of teachers have requested more training and follow-
up, but nothing has happened. And frankly, I sometimes feel like we are
trying to "keep up with the Joneses," and all of this technology really isn't
improving much, as far as I can see.

Principal: We can't have you or anyone else not using this technology in
the classroom. If the superintendent comes around to visit, she will expect to
see these whiteboards in use in every classroom, which is what I expect to
happen in my school.

Teacher: Even if it is not part of the lesson?

Principal: Everyone else in the school is using this technology, and I
expect you to learn it and apply it.

Teacher: But you didn't answer my question!

Principal: I will try to get you some help, but in the meantime, please be a team player and make this a part of your daily instruction.

From this conversation, the principal has made it very clear what is important to him (everyone using the technology all of the time), what he values (compliance), and what he believes (this is *his* school, and he is in charge). From the symbolic perspective, the teacher will now interpret the meaning of this conversation—probably sharing it with colleague who will do the same—and then act upon it. The principal will most likely do the same: figure out the meaning of what was just said and then act upon it from his perspective (perhaps go visit the teacher's classroom again, or maybe provide the teacher with some support as requested).

It is very clear that most, if not all, actions by the school leader can be viewed through a symbolic perspective—from both the leader and the followers. Tasks that may be considered routine by the school leader may, in fact, be perceived by some in this manner, but to others such tasks may be perceived as being of the utmost importance (or of no importance!). In addition, such tasks can be used by the school leader to model behaviors for staff and students, to emphasize core beliefs and values, and to legitimize everyone's role in the success for all.

One way to have a leader reflect upon the symbolic nature of their leadership is to "take a walk" through a typical day. Imagine, for a moment, an invisible person/thing was to follow you around and take notes about what the leader does and the messages that are being sent. It should not surprise those who do this activity at the number of symbolic messages that are being both sent and received, as well as the way they are interpreted and acted upon.

- *Clothing*: The school leader is always "on the stage," and thus, what the leader wears and, to a certain extent, how the leader looks can be an indicator of how the leader feels about herself or himself. The leader is sending a message by the clothes he wears. Some "old-school" leaders may dress professionally with a suit each day to support the message that "as educators, we are professionals, need to be treated as professionals, and thus, we need to act (dress) like professionals."

  Unfortunately, to a certain extent there may still be a double standard when it comes to how school leaders dress, particularly with gender. A female superintendent shared a story about how she spent a lot of money and time on looking professional at all times. She bought clothes that were of top quality and tailored, her shoes were stylish, and she jogged daily in the early morning. Yet she felt that there were multiple interpretations of this, including that "she was better than others," "so that's where her salary (our tax dollars) goes," and "now we see how she got this job."

Ironically, many of these messages she felt were from other females. Her thoughts on all of this: "Look good, take care of yourself, but don't look too good."

- *Cars*: When the leader arrives at the school/district office, two symbolic aspects come into play. First, what kind of car does the leader drive, and what message does it send? While the selection of a car is certainly a personal choice and should not be the business of others, unfortunately it can be. Certainly, if a superintendent is driving an expensive, late-model imported car and the district is in the middle of severe budget issues, including potential layoffs, people throughout the district—employees, parents, and community members—may interpret this in multiple ways, and then, act accordingly.

    A second symbolic aspect is, Where does the leader park? Is there a parking spot—usually closest to the building—that says: *Parking space reserved for superintendent of schools* (or principal of the school)? How do others interpret this, and what impact does this have, particularly in an educational setting? If there is such a designated space and staff are to arrive by 8:00 a.m., what message is there when the leader's car is not there yet?

    One superintendent shared that when he became a superintendent (three different districts), one of things he would do is have the maintenance staff remove *all* reserved parking signs from the district office as well as at each school. And at the first meeting of all principals, teachers, and district staff, he would announce the removal of the signs, saying that "we are all in this together, and while we may have different titles and different salaries, I want everyone to feel a sense of equality and equity when they come to work. So the reserved parking signs are gone." [Pause]. "If you want the prime parking spot, it's now first come, first served."

- *The Leader's Office*: More times than not, the school leader has the prime office in the building, sometimes designated by the only air conditioning unit in the building attached to one of the outer windows! When someone comes into the leader's office, what kind of message is being sent? How is the office decorated? Are there examples of student work? Faculty accomplishments?

    Or, is the office adorned with only the leader's accomplishments, including framed degrees, plaques, and pictures? Just as important, what does the leader do when a person arrives for a conversation? Stand up? Smile? Greet? Stay seated? Frown? Does the leader's demeanor change, according to who the visitor is?

    Todd Whitaker has often said that when people came to his office—especially if they were upset (teachers or parents)—the first thing he would do is stand up, smile, welcome them, and as soon as they sat down, he would bring his chair from behind his desk and place it right next to the visitors. The symbolism here was that the leader's desk can be a huge obstacle to having a productive conversation, and by removing it and sitting closer to the visitors it can reduce tension and negative feelings.

- *Core Beliefs, Mission, and Vision*: These three statements can become the foundation for the success of the school district/school. Or, they can be hung in places in which little if any attention is paid. Some may just collect dust in some file. However, in successful situations, the school leader uses these statements as "the torch and filter" of everything that is important.

  The school leader, in addressing faculty, students, parents, and community, will always bring these statements ("the torch") into the conversation, making these statements "living and breathing," and never allowing them to get too far away. In addition, when there are decisions of importance to be made, these statements are used as "the filter" to align such decisions to the statements.

  In the building, where are these statements located? How often and to what extent are they referred to? During times of debate and perhaps conflict, to what degree are these statements brought into the conversation? If a visitor were to randomly select members of the staff (and students in a school) and ask them to describe these statements, how effectively could they accomplish this?

- *Time*: So how does a school leader spend his or her time? An educational manager is more likely to spend his time doing tasks, solving problems, completing paperwork, and generally staying in his office doing "important stuff." On the other hand, the educational leader is out visiting classrooms (schools) for extended periods of time, modeling great teaching, and emphasizing the teaching-learning context. So there are two issues about time: How does the leader spend his or her time, and how do the followers perceive the leader spending his or her time?

  The school leader, who walks around and visits for a minute here and there, does not develop the same integrity as the leader who takes the time, spends the time, and reflects on the time. Teachers appreciate the leader who spends "real time" in their classrooms. How a leader spends his time is very reflective of his priorities.

  As one superintendent shared, "I cherished the times I went to visit schools. I wish I could have done it more. To lie on the floor with kindergarteners or try experiments in a chemistry class was what I thought I should be doing. When I did that, everyone was glad I was there . . . and it verified that I was supposed to be the 'instructional leader' for the school district. But the board and others really wanted me to be back at the office doing 'superintendent stuff.'"

- *Communication*: As the world—including education—becomes more technology driven, the ability to communicate—speak, write, listen—is often determined by how quickly and concisely a message can be delivered. Telephone calls are often replaced by text messages, meetings that were once face to face are held via computer video programs, and the written word is often replaced with three-or-four-letter chat abbreviations. In addition, people are demanding immediate responses, especially when an issue is considered "urgent" to them.

Several school leaders shared how they respond to this changing communication paradigm. One principal said that she has enlisted the "twenty-four-hour rule" for communication to staff and parents. She promises to respond to every telephone call and email/text she receives within twenty-four hours—unless, of course, it is an emergency.

Another principal stated that he still likes to write handwritten notes to faculty and staff. According to this principal, "I think writing short notes to people and placing them in their mailbox sends a message that I care, that I recognize, and that I took the time to put it in words."

Finally, a superintendent decided to become more open to the staff and the public. Each Thursday, from 3:00 p.m. to 6:00 p.m., he "moves" his office to the main foyer of the district's administration office, and invites people to come visit. He calls it "Coffee and Conversation with the Superintendent." A pot of coffee, bottled water, and some healthy snacks are provided, as well as comfortable chairs for visitors. According to the superintendent, it took time for this idea to become successful, but most weeks, he has between five and ten visitors. Some of the visitors have questions, and others may have problems they want solved. Some are angry or upset, but most appreciate the opportunity to share. But the key to this, according to the superintendent, is not only taking the time but to be a real listener, and afterward, follow up.

• *Building Appearance*: A famous football coach once said, "You are what your record says you are." Some suggest that perhaps the most symbolic feature of a school (and the leadership thereof) is the physical appearance of the school itself. To many, there is nothing more depressing and negative than to drive up to a school (old or new) that may have graffiti on the walls, shrubs and bushes that are unattended, or litter strewn about. As mentioned earlier, the message being sent could be, "Does anyone care? Is anyone in charge?" and both can be perceived as a lack of leadership and priorities.

Similar interpretations can occur inside the building as well, particularly the hallways, the cafeteria (especially after lunches are finished for the day), and bathrooms. One superintendent stated that one of the first places he would visit in the school with the principal would be the student bathrooms. He would then provide his assessment of the cleanliness and appearance of the bathrooms to the principal. It did not take long for the student bathrooms throughout the district to take on a much more pleasant appearance. He stated, "We need school leaders who can manage the building, and cleanliness and neatness—or the lack thereof—sends the wrong message to staff, students, and parents—and to me, about priorities."

• *Faculty Meetings*: Most, if not all, schools have regularly scheduled faculty meetings. Some principals have them weekly, others monthly. The preferred day seems to be Monday and after school, and for the most part, the agenda for the meeting is put together by the principal and is a list of announcements, matters to be attended to, perhaps some sharing of success, and perhaps some recognition. Most of the communication is one way: from principal to faculty.

Whether it is because of the time of day (after school), the day itself (Monday), or the format, these types of meetings do not seem to generate much enthusiasm or interaction. The message is that we have a list of things to do, let's do them and then go home. Oftentimes, one can observe faculty members correcting papers, surfing the Internet on their laptops or cell phones, or even having small conversations. Some principals, however, have decided to change the faculty meeting to a more learner-centered format, where teaching and learning—the core of what the school is about—is the focus. One principal stated,

> First of all, we now have our faculty meetings on Wednesday mornings, from 7:00 a.m. until 8:30 a.m. We have volunteers to watch the early student arrivals in the cafeteria, and in return for coming in early once a week, teachers can leave fifteen minutes earlier every day.
>
> In preparation for this meeting, I send out a list of announcements, upcoming events, and other items the day before, with the message being, if you have any questions or concerns about any of these, we will discuss them from 8:15 to 8:30 at the meeting.
>
> The entire faculty meeting is run by our instructional leadership team, which is made up of five teachers and me . . . we all have one vote. The only caveat is that the meeting must focus on instructional matters, such as sharing best practices, resolving issues, and presenting action research or book studies. Since teaching is the core of what we do, I really feel that teaching and learning should be the focus of these meetings—and that is the message that is being sent over and over.

Since teaching and learning is at the core of schools, symbolic leaders can enable a culture based upon this to be built and sustained through a multitude of actions and messages. Regardless of whether such actions and messages are intentional or not, the sender and the receivers try to make sense of them, and respond accordingly. Symbolic leadership helps both leaders and followers to understand and demonstrate the mission of the school, what is valued, and what is expected.

Yet as presented in this chapter, symbolic leadership is often misunderstood or misapplied. Some school leaders haven't learned about the critical nature of this part of leadership, and may miss opportunities to send a much-needed message in a manner that encourages deeper thought and reflection. Or perhaps the unknowing school leader may send a message in a particular way that ends up having an adverse impact or unintended consequence.

Though it may be intimidating to some leaders, it may be wise to consider that everything that a leader does, says, or acts upon sends a message that can be interpreted in many different ways. The savvy leader always considers such as she leads. Consider the following as it relates to the nature of symbolic leadership:

> Everything that is made beautiful and fair and lovely is made for the eye of one who sees.
> —Rumi

Chapter Three

From Chrysalis to Butterfly

It should be borne in mind that there is nothing more difficult to manage or more doubtful of success or more dangerous to handle than to take the lead in introducing a new order of things.

For the innovator has enemies in all those who are doing well under the old order, and only lukewarm defenders in all those who would do well under the new order.

Thus it happens that whenever his enemies have the opportunity to attack the innovator, they do so with zeal so that the innovator is put in danger.

—Niccolo Machiavelli (1469–1527)[1]

THE DILEMMA OF SCHOOL LEADERSHIP AND CHANGE

As a teacher for more than thirty years, I was involved in many professional development days. Typical of these sessions was the look on the faces of many teachers (including mine) as they sat through yet another session. From apathy and disillusionment to fatigue and boredom, teachers, for the most part, did not find these sessions to be productive and worthwhile. Some teachers would resort to correcting papers, reading the newspaper, or doing crossword puzzles. The worst of these sessions was when they would last the entire day!

For me, even more disappointing was the tone of such sessions. Regardless of the topic, here was an "expert" from the outside telling us about the "newest and greatest" idea to improve both teaching and student achievement. That this expert, who may or may not have any idea about our curriculum, our instruction, our schools, or our students, was telling us what was wrong with us and how it could be fixed!

The expert would stand in front with overhead transparencies, sometimes VHS videos, and of course lots of handouts (which of course were very thick and not available ahead of time). And of course, the delivery of the content by the expert invariably would be in a manner that was exactly how we were told *not* to teach. Standing off to the side would be somebody from central office with a stern look on their face, arms folded, shaking their head in agreement with everything the expert was saying, and making sure everyone was on task.

Most of the time, the message was that we were in the "greatest profession in the world" and that we should be commended for choosing teaching as our vocation. But as "the data shows," we weren't getting the results we needed in terms of student achievement. And if we would only teach the subject "this way with this program, we would all see dramatic results in a short time." The expert had all of the data needed to back up these claims!

So, the solution was simple: all we had to do was change! "Relax," the expert would say, "change is good." More times than not, we would sit through a day—perhaps several days—of this concept. We would then be told to go back to our classrooms and try it. Sometimes, our principal would mandate that we do this, and that he or she would be around soon to visit and observe. Yet looking back, did much really change? For the better? I wonder.

The landscape of education is littered with the "new and best" ideas to transform teaching and learning, including phonics, whole-language, learning activity plans, site-based management, performance-based assessments, direct instruction, team planning, integrating technology, differentiated instruction, curriculum mapping, cross-curriculum planning, and so forth.

Arguably, education has been the target of more reform movements since than 1980s than any other institution in the nation. Beginning with *A Nation at Risk*, followed by Goals 2000, then No Child Left Behind, Race to the Top, and most recently, the move to the Common Core, schools are besieged with the message emphasizing deficits: what is wrong with teaching and learning. Add the financial incentives provided by the federal and state governments for schools to buy into the new and better ideas, as well as sanctions for those who continue to "fail," and there exists a "perfect storm" of apathy and resistance to change.

Yet some schools need to change. In addition to standardized test scores, there is plenty of data available to strongly suggest that hundreds—maybe thousands—of schools across the American landscape are not being successful. And these schools are not just found in high poverty, urban areas. There are plenty of schools in the suburbs and rural areas of the country that are getting the same results as they always have, yet should be doing a lot better.

In many, if not all, of these schools there will be all of the latest technology (e.g., whiteboards, computers), but in how many of these classes is this technology used the same way as overhead projectors and film strips were used a generation ago? And even if the change is going to make things better for both teachers and students, there is still resistance, since the targets of the change and the beneficiaries of the change are the same.

So when it becomes apparent that change is necessary, what is a school leader to do? Do something and get resistance. Do nothing and get the same results. Find a happy medium and maybe something will change. There are literally thousands of books in the market that discuss the change process within the educational context. A lot is based upon the business model of strategic analysis (Where have we been? Where are we now? Where do we want to be in five years? How do we get there? What needs to change for us to get there? Now go and do it!).

Effective change doesn't just happen because a school leader wants it. Nor does it necessarily happen by having the change mandated. It takes a special kind of school leader who is devoted to understanding the emotions, beliefs, ethics, principles, and aspirations of the followers in order to elevate and inspire everyone in the school (including the leader) to accomplish beyond expectations. Such leaders inspire and motivate, have very high standards for themselves and others, emulate such standards, challenge themselves and others to be creative and innovative, and engage with the followers in a personal and individualized manner.

James MacGregor Burns (1978) described this type of leadership as transformational:

> Such leadership occurs when one or more persons engage with others in such a way that leaders and followers raise one another to higher levels of motivation. Transforming leadership ultimately becomes moral in that it raises the level of human conduct and ethical aspiration of both leader and led, and thus it has a transforming effect on both.[2]

Tichy and Devanna (1986, 1990) examined the role of the leader in this transformational process, particularly how a leader can successfully carry out change within the vortex of both internal and external conditions that may impede any chance for success. Tichy and Devanna found that such leaders have traits such as courage, strong belief in people, being value-driven, passionate, persistent, and having vision. In addition, they identified three stages of change that a leader should facilitate. They stated:

> As we watch organizations struggle with the need to change, the developmental sequence bears remarkable similarity to a three-act play. We've chosen to use this theatrical metaphor throughout the book, since it provides an easy way to remember and use the framework for understanding a complex phenomenon:

Act 1. Recognizing the Need for Revitalization. The first act of the drama
centers on the challenges the leader encounters as he or she attempts to alert
the organization to growing threats from the environment.
Act 2. Creating a New Vision. The second act of the drama involves the
leader's struggle to focus the organization's attention on a vision of the future
that is exciting and positive.
Act 3. Institutionalizing Change. In the third and final act of the drama the
leader seeks to institutionalize the transformation so that it will survive his or
her tenure. [3]

Kouzes and Posner (1992, 2012) suggest a leader needs to be an exemplar
for others to observe, such as searching both within the organization and
venturing outside the organization for better ways to be successful. Challenging the process is the means by which the leader pursues opportunities to
innovate and improve.

They argue that the leader will need to encourage others to innovate as
well, yet within an environment that acknowledges that attempting new
methods may not always succeed. When success does not occur, the experience can be used as an opportunity for all to learn, to share, and to grow.
Finally, the leader will need to have an understanding and respect for the
culture and context in which the change is being considered—not forcing
change onto others for the sake of change itself.

Kouzes and Posner state:

> Change is the work of leaders. It's what they do. They are always looking for
> ways to continuously improve, to grow, and to innovate. They know that the
> way things are done today won't get the people to the tomorrow they envision.
> So they experiment. They tinker. They shake things up. They ask, "Where are
> we experimenting and how are we changing?" [4]

Change can mean different things to different people, a point that leaders
sometimes overlook. In fact, Evans (1996) submits, as do many scholars, that
those on the receiving end of change often view change in terms of loss
(losing something dear and close; something one has experienced for a long
time), challenging self-worth (feeling inadequate, insecure, and incompe-
tent), creating confusion (removes clarity, predictability, and rationality), and
causing various levels of conflict (some may "win" from the change, while
others may "lose").

Furthermore, Evans proposed this concept in terms of how people understand the meaning of change, from both the architect of the change to the
receivers. Often, the architect is excited, enthused, and inspired to move
ahead. On the other hand, the receivers may look at the proposed change as
an "unprovoked attack" on who they are, what they do, and what they stand
for. Evans submits:

The different meanings change has for its advocates and targets mirrors a fundamental division within each of us, between our overt embrace of change and our conservative inner impulse to resist it. We can observe this whether change is desired or opposed, planned or unplanned, individual or institutional, and we can see that it afflicts the advocates of change as well as the targets. However, this ambivalence is natural, necessary, and even vital to adaptation. Ambivalence—especially resistance—needs to be seen as part of the solution, not just part of the problem; it demands the attention and respect of all who seek innovation.[5]

One of the most influential scholars of the past two decades regarding leadership and the change process has been John Kotter. In his seminal work *Leading Change* (2012), Kotter proposes an eight-stage process that, in reality, is a series of "projects within projects."[6] The steps are:

1. Establishing a Sense of Urgency
2. Creating the Guiding Coalition
3. Developing a Vision and Strategy
4. Communicating the Change Vision
5. Empowering Employees for Broad-Based Action
6. Generating Short-Term Wins
7. Consolidating Gains and Producing More Change
8. Anchoring New Approaches in the Culture

While some may contend such a linear approach is not advisable for such an unpredictable process, Kotter submits that these steps are in fact, a multi-stage methodology that "is associated with the driving forces behind the process: leadership, leadership, and still more leadership."[7] Leadership matters and may matter the most when leading an organization through the change process.

A critical factor during the change process is the degree to which the school leader can provide motivation, support, and guidance without having to be in control of everything that everyone will be doing. Oftentimes, this is much easier said than done, particularly if the change initiative is their idea. Fullan (2008) characterizes this as the "too tight–too loose dilemma." He proposes that if the school leader is "too tight"—inflexible, demanding, overly structured—then some followers may become resistant. Or others may "just fall in line," complete the task, and move on. Either way, imagination and creativity will suffer.

On the other hand, if the school leader is "too loose"—detached, laissez-faire, disconnected—followers may feel detached and not supported, and ultimately begin to lose interest in the initiative.

Fullan proposes purposeful peer interaction, which is the balance point between too tight and too loose. Within this context, the leader's role is to provide conditions in which those who are involved in the process have the opportunity to inquire, to share, to learn, and to experiment in a meaningful, collaborative, and supportive manner. According to Fullan,

> Leaders should seek to create prosocial environments populated by prosocial individuals. Prosocials are not passive do-gooders. They do not simply go along with the crowd.
> They are committed to getting important things done.
> Further, you [the leader] should stand for a high purpose, hire talented individuals, create mechanisms for purposeful peer interaction with a focus on results, and stay involved but avoid micromanaging. Put differently, once you establish the right conditions and set the process in motion, trust the process and the people in it. [8]

The significance of what these and other scholars are suggesting is that change theory, when applied in a manner that is true to theory and practice, actually works! And just as important, leadership really matters! There are plenty of studies and stories of leaders and their schools progressing through the maze of change and, in the end, being highly successful!

Such success is not just for schools that are rich with resources and talented faculty; examples of successful change initiatives can be seen that cross socioeconomic lines, racial and cultural lines, and geographic lines. So the question becomes, Why do some schools succeed in changing for the better, and most don't?

The first element to consider is who is actually leading the change. History is full of examples of leaders who have successfully implemented change, which ultimately have led to a successful transformation of a nation, of industries, of organizations, and schools as well.

The names of Abraham Lincoln, Mustafa Kemal Ataturk, Mohandas Gandhi, and Nelson Mandela are part of a long list of leaders who have dramatically changed a nation. During the last hundred-plus years, people such as Henry Ford and recently, Steve Jobs and Bill Gates have played a significant role in transforming a particular industry from what it once was and what it then became. And there are many other exemplary leaders who have done similar things within quite different and unique cultures and organizations around the world. Thus, it becomes critical to examine why those leaders and others have succeeded when many, many others have failed.

A second element to explore is the reason behind the change. Some may posit that change is inevitable, and the leader just might happen to be in the right place at the opportune time. Others suggest that the leader may see a need for change, and using a position of authority, attend to the process.

Still, leaders may be forced to change the way things are due to pressures from outside. Examples here include voters demanding changes, boards who oversee organizations may direct the leader to change, and legislation from local, state, or federal agencies may mandate certain changes. An example of the latter in education was the passage and implementation of the No Child Left Behind law of 2002, in which the federal government of the United States began an unprecedented involvement in the thousands of public schools across the nation.

Furthermore, it is also important to understand the suggested change in terms of the leader's role and values with respect to the appropriateness of certain actions that will influence the process and ultimate transformation. One could argue that both Adolf Hitler and Joseph Stalin are examples of leaders who completely transformed their own nation, but at a huge cost to the lives of millions of people, their culture, and way of life. And ultimately, what was built eventually was destroyed.

Even if the despots are left out of the conversation, what does it take for a leader to create conditions that will allow for change to be successfully implemented and sustained?

Two stories are now presented. One story is about the transformation of a group of people by a young lawyer in a foreign nation, followed by the story of how a new school leader initiates the transformation of a high school.

COURAGE, HONOR, AND SELF-SACRIFICE

Mr. Ally and I who have come as a Deputation from the Transvaal on behalf of the British Indians, venture to request an appointment with you in order to enable us to place the British Indian position in the Transvaal before you. We shall be extremely obliged if you could spare a short time to enable us to wait on you.

Your humble servant,
M. K. Gandhi
[letter to Winston Churchill, colonial undersecretary, November 1906] [9]

Mohandas Gandhi had been back in South Africa for three years. Several years prior, Gandhi had returned to his native India, disillusioned and disappointed. His work and leadership in support of fighting discrimination against Indians living in South Africa had not resulted in any significant improvements over the past decade, and he felt that it was a "lost cause." But friends had begged Gandhi to reconsider, and reluctantly, he did return to South Africa.

Gandhi had first come to South Africa in 1893, at the age of twenty-four, as a lawyer representing the Muslim Indian Traders in Pretoria. At that time, there were a little over fifty thousand Indians in the Natal region of South Africa. Of these, one-third was "indentured laborers" in plantations, mines, and railways who had been brought on five-year contracts with the promise of land and rights at the end of indenture. About thirty thousand were "free Indians"—those who had completed indenture and their children—and five thousand belonged to the trading community, forced to live in squalor conditions and as targets of legalized discrimination, with few political, economic, or social rights.

In the mid-1890s, Gandhi was unsuccessful in leading an attempt to keep a law from being passed that would prevent Indians in South Africa from voting. However, Gandhi's efforts brought significant attention to these and other injustices that his fellow Indians faced. It also brought notoriety to Gandhi as well.

During this time, Gandhi himself was often the target of discrimination and violence, as was the case with most Indians living there at the time. He was thrown off a train in Pietermaritzburg after refusing to move from the all-white, first-class section. When Gandhi began to question authorities about the conditions that Indians were subjected to in South Africa, he became a target of attacks and beatings.

Thus, the early years of the twentieth century provided a defining era for Gandhi, in that his experiences, as well as those of other Indians in South Africa, would become the foundation for his lifelong journey into activism against social injustice. In addition, Gandhi began to question his place, as well as that of all Indians, in a society monopolized by the British. Sometimes, change comes from outside in. Other times, it comes from inside out. What was to happen next would be change from both within and without, for both Gandhi and Indians.

In August 1906, the Colonial Office of the British government in South Africa declared that every Indian resident in Transvaal over the age of eight would be required to register and be fingerprinted. According to the government, this law was needed to keep track of immigrants from India. To some Indians, particularly those in London, it did not seem to be a big issue; the larger issue was the question of independence for India.

Gandhi was angered and felt insulted by this law, which was referred to by Indians in South Africa as the "Black Act." Not only did Gandhi feel that this law was unfair and targeted at one group (Indians in South Africa), he also was angered as to why the only two groups in South Africa required to be fingerprinted were Indians and criminals.

What happened next was a transformational moment for not only Gandhi but Indians in South Africa and India as well. On September 11, 1906, the Hamidia Islamic Society organized a protest meeting to voice their opposition to the "Black Act." The more than three thousand were jammed into an auditorium in Johannesburg, including Muslims and Hindus, merchants and street people, the wealthy and the untouchables. When it was Gandhi's turn to speak, he asked every Indian in South Africa to refuse to be fingerprinted or registered, even if it meant they would lose their jobs or be sent to prison. Gandhi stated:

> We might have to go to gaol [prison], where we might be insulted. We might have to go hungry and suffer extreme heat or cold. Hard labour might be imposed on us. We might be flogged by rude warders. We might be fined heavily and our property might be attached and held up to auction . . . Opulent today, we might be reduced to abject poverty tomorrow. We might be deported. Suffering from starvation and similar hardships in gaol, some of us might fall ill and die. In short, therefore, it is not at all impossible that we might have to endure every hardship that we can imagine, and wisdom lies in pledging ourselves on the understanding that we shall have to suffer all that is worst.[10]

Over the next few months, Gandhi began to implement a movement against the law that would be the foundation for action against the British Empire for the rest of his life. It would be referred to as Satyagraha, which translated means "truth force" and implies passive resistance, strength, and discipline to a nonviolent cause of action.

Significant changes began to occur. Numerous nonviolent, passive-resistant demonstrations occurred throughout Transvaal. Indians refused to be fingerprinted. They refused to be registered. Some who were registered publicly burned their cards. Demonstrators, including Gandhi, were beaten and jailed. Yet the demonstrations did not stop. The more the British used force, the more Gandhi and his supporters resisted. While it took almost two years, a compromise was eventually agreed upon.

Gandhi would return to India in 1915. By that time, his life had been transformed, as has those who had been with him throughout the struggles in South Africa. He struggled with his public notoriety, in that he did not want this struggle for Indian respect and independence be viewed as "Gandhi's movement." What he wanted was an "all-Indian movement." Yet at the same time, he recognized that, through Satyagraha, he had nothing to hide. He would not fear inquiry or investigation. Such openness and devotion would help Gandhi inspire, motivate, challenge, engage, and eventually uplift the people of India and lead them to a place where they had never been or expected to be.

WHEN GOOD IS NOT GOOD ENOUGH

> Going into this job, I knew a number of things were against me. I would be the first and only female high school principal among the twelve high schools within the district. I was an outsider—from a different state! I was replacing the beloved principal who had opened the high school twenty years ago. I knew if I was too assertive, then the "b-word" would be attached to me. If I

wasn't assertive, then I would be easy pickings and people would walk all over me. And finally, the school was already considered a good high school!

It was the late 1980s. Ellen Gregory had a PhD in Educational Leadership. She had been a biology teacher for fifteen years before taking a leave to work on her doctorate. When Ellen came back to the district with her degree, she was assigned the position of director of secondary curriculum and instruction. While she became very competent at her position, she missed the vibrancy and excitement of being in a school. Ellen then became an assistant principal. After five years in this position, Ellen began to look for school principal vacancies.

Ellen interviewed for several positions and was even offered a position of assistant principal at the school where she had taught—a lateral move that was tempting since it was at her old school. But that was not what she wanted. While very well respected at her former school, Ellen really wanted to start anew. It didn't take long, for Ellen applied for and was named the principal of Northwestern High School, beginning with the 1990 school year.

When Northwestern High School opened in 1970, most of the area was rural. A majority of students either lived on farms or in the village of Williamsburg. There were only four high schools in the county at this time. Enrollment at the high school was eight hundred for grades nine through twelve.

Yet over the next twenty years, much changed. People from the suburbs began moving out to Williamsburg. Farms turned into housing developments. Shopping centers opened. Two-lane highways leading into the village became crowded with commuters leaving for work in the morning and returning in the evening. Fast food restaurants began to spring up.

Despite all of the change going on within the community, Northwestern High School remained relatively stable. While the student enrollment more than doubled to almost 1,800 students by 1990, the teachers and students continued to be successful. SAT scores and graduation rates were relatively high, discipline issues were nothing more than ordinary, and most students participated in many different extracurricular activities.

Much of the credit for this was given to David Edwards, the long-time principal of the school. Over the twenty years that he was principal, he was able to hire teachers, coaches, advisors, and even custodians that fit his image of what a high school should be: a place where students are safe and have opportunities to grow into young adults. David was very conservative and traditional in the values he placed on education, and led the school in such a manner. He was respected by all and loved by many. And he was retiring at the end of the 1989 to 1990 school year.

Enter Dr. Ellen Gregory, the new principal of Northwestern High School. When the board of education announced her as the principal, the faculty was less than enthusiastic. Some wondered why the board went outside of the district when it could have promoted one of the current assistant principals. Others were concerned that there was some sort of agenda in bringing someone in from the outside. They asked, "If it's not broken, why change?" And to some of the male faculty, there were concerns about whether or not a female could actually lead such a big high school. One long-time male coach reportedly said, "I'll give her two years max—this place will run her over."

Ellen knew that this was not going to be easy. She had seen other school leaders come into schools and try force their agenda. And more times than not, this was not a recipe for success. So Ellen decided that, at least for the first year, she would spend most of her time learning about the school—the teachers, the students, and the community.

At her first faculty meeting in late August, Ellen was introduced to the staff by the assistant superintendent of administrative services. Ellen would later reflect that the "silence was deafening" when she addressed the staff. After some preliminary remarks, Ellen did inform the faculty that she would visit every teacher's classroom for at least one full period by Thanksgiving. She said these visits would not be evaluative, but more of a way for her to find out how teachers teach and students learn here at Northwestern High School. Ellen then said she would repeat the process from early January to the spring break. And then, she would share what she learned.

Good on her word, Ellen visited every teacher's classroom twice by the spring break of her first year. In the beginning, some teachers were put off by having the principal come in to their classrooms, while others were happy to have Ellen in their class. Ellen made sure that visits occurred at all times— even first thing on Monday, last thing on Friday, and all times in between.

To her credit, unless there was an obvious issue of great magnitude, Ellen did not make any of these visits evaluative. She took notes, walked around and spoke with students, and invited teachers to stop by and share thoughts. Some teachers did, most didn't. Some praised her for being so visible, while others thought she should be in the office, taking care of "principal stuff."

It was at a staff meeting in April that Ellen presented the results of her visits. She provided the staff with an overview of her 180 visits (two per teacher), making certain that no individual teacher or department was identified. Ellen then provided the raw data from her visits in a spreadsheet format.

During two faculty meetings, departments were given the opportunity to analyze and synthesize the data and to discuss, debate, and reflect upon it as well. At the end of the second meeting, each department was asked to present their thoughts. The following was a list of common thoughts that were presented by the departments:

- For the most part, teachers use structured lesson plans, per the district-approved format.
- Students are generally well behaved and attentive in class.
- Teachers are enthusiastic and positive.
- Most of the instruction is teacher directed; students are passive learners, mostly taking notes and responding to teacher-led discussions and questioning; in addition, student time-on-task begins to decrease from about the halfway point of the class to the end.
- For required courses, the school has three tracks: high, average, and challenging. Students in the challenging track (lower ability) are taught in a much more rote manner than students in the other two tracks, and there are more discipline issues found in this track as well.
- Friday seems to be "test" day at the school. Such tests are teacher made and consist of objective questions (multiple choice, true-false) and/or essays. Performance assessments were evident only in very few instances.
- Within the framework of the current forty-five-minute class period, there is little time for beginning the class with any type of anticipatory/motivational activities; nor at the end of class, time is rarely used to summarize and assess student learning.
- Homework is given on a regular basis, yet there didn't seem to be consistency in how often it would be given, how and when it would be graded, and what type of follow-up would occur.
- Both students and teachers appear to be in a "hurried" state of going from one class to another.
- Teachers rarely have time to collaborate on common planning, and there does not seem to be much interest or knowledge of such planning within departments or across departments.

A number of the teachers were not very happy with the "critical" nature of the data, but overall, Ellen was happy with the quality of the discussion, particularly with the fact that the list was generated by the teachers themselves, based upon the data. The overall sentiment was that there were three issues that needed to be addressed for overall improvement: (1) more time for planning and collaboration; (2) less hurried schedule for teachers and students; (3) professional development for time management and improving teacher-student interaction.

It was at this time that a relatively new concept was gaining momentum in a few states, particularly Colorado and Virginia. The concept was called "block scheduling" and was a way for high schools to address many of the items that Ellen and her staff had identified. Each of the high schools within the district, including Northwestern High School, had a traditional eight-period day, with each class being approximately forty-five minutes. For the most part, each class would meet for the entire 180 days.

However, with the "block scheduling" concept, schools were being organized into a four-period day, with each class being ninety minutes. Two models were emerging from the schools in neighboring states: one model was that individual classes would meet every other day for the entire year; the other was a semester model in which students would take four classes every day for a semester and then would take four different classes the next semester.

According to those few schools who were doing this, the day was less hurried, students were not overwhelmed with "eight different teachers who rarely talked with each other," and there appeared to be much more collaboration among teachers. Under this model, teachers would teach three classes per day (instead of five or six) of ninety minutes each and have ninety minutes of planning.

Ellen thought that this concept was very interesting and might not only address the issues identified but also transform Northwestern High School from a good high school to a school of excellence. So Ellen began researching the concept, making phone calls, and even visiting two schools in a nearby state that were involved in block scheduling. By the middle of the summer, Ellen was convinced that this was the way to go.

But she also knew that if this became known as "Ellen's idea," it would not have a very good chance of succeeding. She was well aware of change theory and why most changes do not succeed. Leadership, support, and not rushing an initiative were all critical to the success or failure.

One of the first people she engaged with was Rob Wolf, department chair for the English department, a coach, advisor for clubs, and one of the most highly respected and well-liked members of the staff. Always innovative and creative in the classroom, Rob jumped at the chance to be part of this. So the two of them spent much of the summer finding out as much as they could about block scheduling.

At the same time, Ellen was in contact with the both the superintendent of schools and the assistant superintendent for curriculum and instruction. Both were generally supportive of these first stages, but the superintendent was adamant that if this was to become a reality, there would have to be a faculty vote, with at least 80 percent in support; there would have to be student and parental input; and finally, the board of education would have to formally approve this change. The superintendent told Ellen that the faculty vote would have to occur in December, followed by a formal presentation and approval by the board in mid January. Then, if all goes well, the block-scheduling plan would go into effect the following school year.

During the first faculty meeting prior to the opening of school, Ellen unveiled the concept in very general terms to the staff. She provided the reasons for examining block scheduling, that it was not a "done deal," and that there would be plenty of opportunities for staff to be part of this process.

She then turned the rest of the meeting over to Rob, who explained his role
and what he would be doing throughout the process.

During the month of September, teams of teachers from Northwestern
High School visited schools that were already involved in block scheduling.
Rob Wolf went on each of these visits, but Ellen did not. Each team then
provided their observations at the next faculty meeting.

In addition, Ellen arranged for two groups of teachers from other schools
that had been involved in block scheduling to visit Northwestern High
School. The first group came in early October and the second in mid October. Each group worked for the day with respective departments, and the day
concluded with a faculty meeting "Q & A."

While Rob was "on stage," Ellen worked behind the scenes, trying to
determine who the "fence sitters" were and who the "no-no's" might be. She
spoke regularly with the teachers' union school representative. Ellen invited
members of the PTA to participate in visits to the school. In addition, she and
Rob met with groups of students to discuss the concepts.

In early November, a series of evening meetings with parents were held.
Ellen opened up each meeting with a few remarks, but then turned it over
completely to Rob and his team of teachers and several students for presenta-
tions.

By mid November, the school was abuzz with this concept. Faculty meetings had turned into "learning and sharing" meetings, with Rob facilitating
such. The superintendent attended one of the November faculty meetings as
well. Surveys were sent to parents and students, and results came back very
positive. The faculty then voted, with an overwhelming 90 percent in favor
of moving ahead with this concept.

In January, Ellen and Rob presented the concept and data to the board of
education. The board voted unanimously to let Northwestern High School
implement block scheduling for the following year.

It was now time to start planning, and at the same time, keep the momentum moving forward. During the second semester, small groups of teachers
were allowed to try out "ninety-minute blocks" for a week at a time. School
district curriculum specialists were brought to the school to help with lesson
planning, unit planning, and time management support. A few of the most
skeptical teachers visited some of the schools that others had done in the fall.
It was both a very energizing time for everyone, and at the same time, rather
tense, for no one really knew if this was going to work or not.

As spring moved into summer, Ellen was able to secure professional
development monies for each department to meet during the summer for one
week. It was voluntary on the part of each teacher, but almost seventy of the
teachers participated.

The first faculty meeting of the school year was always held on the last
Thursday of August, precisely at 9:00 a.m. Students will arrive for classes on

the following Monday, unless it is Labor Day; if so, classes begin on Tuesday. At this particular staff meeting, there was a level of anxiety, tension, and excitement that was much more palpable than in other years. Teachers were nervous if they could actually teach ninety-minute classes. Some couldn't wait to get started; others thought about what would happen if this plan didn't work out at all!

Ellen Gregory was nervous as well. She was certain that if this didn't work out, her life as a principal would be short-lived. But then again, she was very confident and kept reminding herself of all the hard work that Rob and the staff had done the last year, and all of the learning that everyone had been involved in. And she was ready to add the "icing to the cake" when she got up to speak.

Ellen welcomed everyone back and thanked them for everything that they had accomplished over the past year. She acknowledged the tension and nervousness, and reminded everyone, that like the big football game, all it would take is a "few hits and we'll be off and running." She then said that the rest of preservice time would be dedicated to getting ready for Monday, including the traditional faculty/staff picnic.

Then Ellen told the staff that she had an announcement to make. The room got very quiet, and she waited for a moment. She then said,

> I want you to know, that beginning next Monday, I will not be available for any principal duties during our first block class, which as you know, will be from 8:00 to 9:30 each morning. All administrative issues, during that time, will be handled by Jim and Tessa, our two assistant principals.
>
> Now, you may be wondering where I will be. First, let me explain to you that what we are asking of each other is truly extraordinary. And we are asking of each other is a lot. So, how could I, in good conscience, ask you to change and me go about my business as usual? I can't and I won't.
>
> So beginning next Monday and for the whole first semester, during first block class, I will be teaching tenth-grade biology!
>
> I want to experience what you are experiencing, and share my experiences with you, and you with me. Only the two assistant principals knew of this in advance—and they were sworn to secrecy. I, too, am anxious and nervous, and yes, very excited. I can't wait for us to get started!

When Ellen finished, there was momentary silence. Some of the faculty began clapping and standing, followed by everyone else in the room. Northwestern High School was ready to start anew!

LEARNING FOR LEADING

At this point, it is worth addressing two questions regarding change. First, what kind of school leadership is most likely to impede or prevent success in the change process? Very simply put—transactional leadership (quid pro quo), selfish leadership (this is all about me), ruthless leadership (my way or the highway), and/or unethical leadership (the end justifies the means) will not work over time. Yes, sometimes this leadership can work for a while. But the successes are short-lived, superficial, and counterproductive. School leaders are strongly advised to avoid a focus on transactional leadership for the change process at all costs!

The second question relates to resistance to change. The school leader's understanding of resistance to change will be critical for the success or failure of the initiative. It is imperative to know that resistant to the proposed change is natural, and is demonstrated in varying ways and to differing levels of intensity. As shown, some of this resistance may be that followers are nervous, timid, and anxious about how the change will impact them.

Some of the resistance may come from those who really believe it is not in the best interest of the school and goes against their own professional beliefs. Still, some of resistance will come from those who might be angry, defiant, and/or resentful. In any case, resistance will occur and the wise leader will not avoid it.

Evans (1996) categorizes people within an organization who are facing change into three groups: Red Hots, Unfreezables, and Cryogenics, based upon two dimensions: commitment to change and ability to change. An exemplary school leader understands, acknowledges, and recognizes where each person is along the spectrum of change, and that this can be critical to the success and longevity of the change process.

- *Red Hots*: those who demonstrate a positive commitment to the change and are also exhibiting the capacity to implement the change successfully. The tendency is to leave these people alone, since they "get it." But that can be dangerous for the leader and the change process because these "high flyers" may: (1) burn out; (2) feel unappreciated; (3) could begin to regress in doing things the old way. The savvy leader understands that leaving this group alone is not a viable option, and that providing support, guidance, and a professional relationship is critical to their continued positive attitude and extraordinary abilities.
- *Unfreezables*: those who demonstrate a positive commitment to the change, but are having difficulty implementing the change (and they may not realize the latter!). Obviously, this group can't be left alone. Ongoing professional development, including mentoring, visiting Red Hots (both within and outside the school), and participating in collaborative teaching are but a few ways to move these people to their next level of expertise. They have the right attitude; all they need now is support, guidance, and some TLC!

- *Cryogenics*: these are the ultimate resistors. Sometimes they can be described as "No-No's," "Naysayers," "Killjoys," and "Prophets of Doom." They are not committed to the change and will do everything in their power to resist the change. They strongly believe they have legitimate reasons to resist this change and would like nothing more than to "tear down" the process, bring others along with them, and if possible, cause the demise of the leader. Then, they can claim victory!

Some school leaders avoid the resistors in hope that they will not be noticed or that they will just disappear. Others may be afraid to confront them. Avoidance is not an option. Most likely, others will notice their behaviors, and they probably won't be leaving very soon. Furthermore, if these people know the leader is frightened of them, they may well "smell blood in the water" and will derive much pleasure in attacking the leader in a covert and/or open manner. Much like sharks in the water, the dangerous resistors may be on the surface, while others are swimming below. Yet they are there, and they can be very dangerous!

On very rare occasions, a small percentage of these resistors may change their attitude and become more positive and accepting of the change. If this happens, the leader needs to be congratulated. But leaders should never assume that this will happen!

This issue, itself, will not go away or go unnoticed. And the longer the school leader avoids this, the more dangerous the situation will become—for both the change process and the leader as well. The rest of the staff will be watching how the leader is or isn't attending to this situation. Subsequently, if nothing is done, this resistance and negativity could spread to other individuals and departments/teams within the school.

Action is necessary! And as difficult as it may be, the leader needs to provide each of the resistors with acknowledgment, support, and guidance. Undoubtedly, this will be time consuming and frustrating for the leader. Yet this is a much better option than doing nothing.

If, after time, the resistance and negativity continues to occur, the school leader will need to confront the resistors. Allowing them to continue along this path is not an option for them or the leader. This is the point when the leader begins the process of "moving this person along," perhaps having the person transferred to another school, dismissed for cause, or at least put on a very structured, outcomes-based individual professional performance plan, which has specific sanctions if the resistance continues.

Yet when faced with change, school leaders will often encounter peculiar and odd situations that on the surface may not make much sense. So even as difficult and challenging as this process can be, there are some specific strategies that a school leader can apply to significantly enhance the chances for success. In preparing for this book, a number of school leaders shared their experiences with the change process, and the ambiguities they faced.

The following are presented as guideposts for the school leader contemplating the change process:

• *Look in the Mirror*. First and perhaps foremost, the school leader should consider having a careful self-analysis of why this change is being considered. This also can be an opportune time to engage with a mentor. Accordingly, questions that need to be addressed can include the following:

- Really, why am I pursuing this change in our school? Am I being pressured into this change? Am I doing this for the greater good or for my own professional good?
- How much do I know about the theory and practice of the change? What do I need to learn? Where can I get this information?
- Which "superstars" on my staff will I engage in the conversation first? And when?
- To what degree have I communicated this plan to my superiors (the principal with the school district office; the superintendent with the board of education)? What is their level of commitment at this point?
- What resources (human, financial, structural) will need to be put in place, not only prior to beginning the process but also throughout?
- What role will I play in this process? Will I be "the sage on the stage or the guide on the side?"
- Self-analysis provides the leader with the opportunity to acutely assess one's commitment and role for this suggested change, as well as to address any gaps or issues. Without doing this, the change process may be in jeopardy before it even gets started!

• *Hurry Up and Slow Down*. Both superintendents and principals often mentioned the issue of time, particularly as it related to implementing a significant change. Buoyed with enthusiasm for the change, some leaders wanted to get the process moving—now! So meetings were held, strategies were put in place, and people were "encouraged" to get on board as soon as possible. Other school leaders decided to take a more gradual, slower pace.

Yet in both cases, these leaders were met with significant resistance, including some who, upon looking back, felt the process was doomed from the beginning. What they learned was that there is no guaranteed time when to start the change process or how best to pace the process. Each setting is unique, including personalities, needs and wants, and culture. One superintendent remarked,

> Go too fast with the process and staff may feel that the light at the end of the tunnel was the train that just ran them over. They will feel overwhelmed and

hesitant to continue. On the other hand, if you move too slowly, staff will begin to lose interest, and any energy built up for this change will most certainly begin to dissipate. As a matter of fact, I have an index card in a drawer in my desk that says the following: "When it comes to change, speed kills and does so forever."

• *Silence Is Deafening.* Some school leaders shared the experience of presenting a change to their staff and shareholders, only to receive silence and a few heads moving up and down. Or, as the process began to be implemented, there would be silence throughout the faculty meeting. Some confessed that they would often take this silence as acceptance: no one is complaining, so it must be working okay. Everyone must be in favor of it, so let's move on.

Reflecting on this, these leaders realized that this lack of response was really revealing something significant, such as disapproval, lack of clarity, or lack of enthusiasm, waiting for a deep conversation. As one principal stated long after an unsuccessful attempt at change,

> They [the teachers] wanted to scream their disapproval of what we were doing and how we were going about it, but, for various reasons, no one would say anything. Some were just naturally quiet. Others were new and didn't feel it was their place. They shook their heads or just said "okay." I completely misread the entire situation—this could have been a "teachable moment(s)," where we could learn from each other, discuss the pros and cons, and more. But instead, we just moved on. And eventually, it became the death of what I thought would really help our school go to the next level.

• *The Abilene Paradox.* Harvey (1988)[11] suggests that people within an organization may make decisions on whether to support the change process not on what they actually want to do but on what they think others may want to do. Thus, the results are that everybody in the organization decides to do something that nobody really wants to do but what they thought everyone else wanted to do!

Unlike the concept of Group Think, in which people will agree with others and feel generally good about their decision, in the Abilene Paradox, people eventually feel bad about what was decided and lament the fact that they actually supported something that they never wanted to begin with. One superintendent, who learned the difficult way about this ambiguity, shared the following:

> So, after more than six months of meetings, research, learning, and discussion, I got the thirty principals together and said that if 80 percent or more voted in favor of the longer school year, we would move ahead with it. The vote was taken, and it was twenty-eight yes, and two no! I was ecstatic. But after that, it really went nowhere. Behind the scenes, there was a lot of bickering and arguing. And eventually it all spilled out in a meeting. One principal after

another pretty much said that they had voted for it—not because they wanted it—but they thought everyone else wanted it! They were afraid of the negative ramifications, from both their peers and me as well. So they just went along with it!

• *The Implementation Dip.* Things are going reasonably well and it appears that the change has taken root. Teachers seem happy, as do the students. As the school leader, you can feel the change in the school's culture. Yet Fullan (2008) warns that this can also be a time in which people may begin to become too comfortable, move into complacency, and even revert back to old ways. Most likely, it won't be a sudden shift, but if left unattended, it can have negative implications.

There is nothing wrong with having members of the staff become comfortable with the change. Being comfortable during the process allows people to learn and try this new way; people will be willing to collaborate and share in a manner that is safe for them; still others will build upon what they are learning and create extensions of the original concept.

Yet sometimes such comfort may lead to complacency, in which some may have reached a level of capacity, satisfaction, and acceptance with their current conditions. Thus, complacency can lead to one having clouded judgment and a false sense of reality in terms of attitude and ability. Without continued inspiration, guidance, support, and opportunities to grow further, some may even begin to go back to "the good old ways" of doing things. And once this occurs, it can easily spread among others.

It can be a mistake to think once the change has been implemented that everything will continue on an upward path. The savvy school leader will anticipate the implementation dip and have appropriate strategies ready to implement to counter a potential decline in performance. Leading and living through a change process is not easy. The leader knows and understands the emotions of the staff—both individual and group—as they venture through this and beyond.

A retired principal, who had led several schools through significant change, offers the following:

> In every situation, I became obsessed with knowing my staff and building relationships. That way, I would know what makes them "tick," both individually and collectively. So any time we went through a change process and it was up and running, I would be extra vigilant . . . looking, talking, walking around . . . trying to get the temperature. And once I got the feeling that things could begin to level off (or were leveling off), it was time for me to "stir the pot," and the level of this would depend on how much the staff needed—some would need more than others. But my other obsession throughout this was that there was no way we were going to go back. No way!

In the end, the change process provokes concerns that may test the boundaries of a leader's ability to influence others within the school. Certainly school leaders can make a difference during the process, but only after they have developed a comprehensive understanding of the current context of the organization and the people. Whether the catalyst for change comes from the outside or from within, successful school leaders see what is happening, what needs to happen, and then devise a plan to ensure its success. Consider the following:

> Like the butterfly, I have the strength and the hope to believe,
> In time, I will emerge from my cocoon . . .
> Transformed.
> —Kirsti Dyer

Chapter Four

Thinking About Thinking

Everything that every effective leader does is sandwiched between action on the ground and thinking in the abstract. Action without thinking is thoughtless; thinking without action is passive. Every leader has to find a way to combine these two mind-sets—to function at the point where thinking meets practical doing.
—Gosling and Mintzberg [1]

At a leadership conference for school principals, one of the sessions was titled, "If You Ask Yourself a Question, What Kind of Answer Do You Get?" Once the participants had taken their seats, the presenter passed out a daily calendar and asked each to take out their phone or tablet. The presenter then requested that everyone take a few moments to write down all of the events that occurred in their schedules for the past three days while they were at school. Once this was completed, the presenter asked them to add any interruptions and/or unscheduled events to the schedule. Once this was completed, the presenter asked the participants to share what they had written down in groups of two or three.

After about five minutes, the presenter asked the entire group the following question:

At what point in your schedule did you take the time to think and reflect upon what had happened or was happening in your school?

At first, there was silence, then some chuckling. Yet the presenter pressed on by asking the same question again. Some of the responses included:

- The only time I get to think is when I am going from Crisis A to Crisis B, and then I usually get intercepted along the way. But reflect . . . can't seem to remember.
- I try to think and reflect on the drive home every night, but most times I have places go, things to get, so it usually doesn't happen.
- Think? Reflect? I can't get to the bathroom most days, let alone take time to think.
- If I ever sat in my office and did some deep thinking and reflection—and someone stopped in unexpectedly—I think the word would get out that I'm either sleeping in my office or not busy getting things done!
- At church on Sunday morning.

School leaders—like leaders in other industries—are often perceived as effective—or not—in terms of how hard they work. Take the school principal as an example. Their car needs to be the first one in the parking lot in the morning and the last to leave in the evening. Meetings all day. Angry parents. Teacher observations. If there is a concert, the leader needs to be there. Same with a sporting event or parent council meeting. Students participating in a STEM competition on Saturday—the principal needs to be there.

For the superintendent, it is very similar. If the district has five high schools, the superintendent needs to attend each of the graduations. Kiwanis Club. Rotary Club. Martin Luther King birthday celebration. The mantra appears to be: Be There, Do It, and Don't Miss It!

The pace and nature of school leadership has significantly changed over the past several decades. The problems of public education are becoming more abstract and puzzling than ever, and the solutions to educational issues of the twenty-first century will not be resolved using the twentieth-century leadership paradigm of "see the problem, solve the problem and move on." School leaders are more likely to concentrate on action but are not skilled at stepping back to think about their actions and situations.

This is not to deny the fact that the school leader needs to be an active leader. Getting important things accomplished, being visible, and ensuring that the organization is heading in the appropriate direction are but a few of the jobs the school leader must attend to. Yet at the same time, perhaps a more passive approach to school leadership is necessary, in the sense that the leader becomes more of a thinker and less of a constant doer. The challenge, therefore, is to create conditions that allow the leader to provide a balanced approach to leading, in which contemplation meets action—before, during, and after the fact.

A number of scholars submit that this type of balance is not occurring within the context of contemporary school leadership. According to Gosling and Mintzberg (2003),[2] leaders may often fall into one of two distinct groups: (1) they concentrate so much on action that they do not provide themselves (or others) the opportunity to think through issues before, during, and after decisions are made; (2) they spend so much time thinking that that nothing seems to be getting accomplished and decisions are being made. Accordingly, the work of the leader becomes a quest to obtain balance between doing and thinking. Margaret Wheatley submits,

> It's hard to look at modern life and see our capacities for meaning-making. We don't use our gifts to be more aware or thoughtful. We're driven in the opposite direction. Things move too fast for us to reflect, demanding tasks give us no time to think, and we barely notice the lack of meaning until forced to stand still by illness, tragedy, or job loss. But in spite of our hurry, we cannot stop life's dynamic of self-reference or the human need for meaning. If we want to influence any change, anywhere, we need to work *with* this powerful process rather than deny its existence.[3]

The answer to the dilemmas presented here might be that leaders need to learn how to become better at thinking through reflection and reflective practice. These concepts are not new; they have been around for centuries, but sometimes they are misunderstood and/or overlooked by those who may need them the most: our school leaders.

REFLECTION AND REFLECTIVE PRACTICE

To some, reflection means nothing more than "to think about something that just happened, and figure out the learned lessons." But true reflection is much more than that. It is a purposeful, deep, and critical way for a leader to think deeply about what is occurring within the context of their leadership.

Reflection, as a way of thinking and learning, can be traced back to Socrates, who constantly challenged his students through inquiry, discussion, and debate. According to Socrates, knowledge is essential to stimulate critical thinking in terms of illuminating ideas, and thus the connection between such knowledge and its outcome can result in more elaborate and creative thinking, with often surprising results!

John Dewey (1933) submits,

> Reflection is much more than quiet thinking over past events. It aims toward a goal such as a set of solutions to dilemmas or problems and understanding them. In pursuit of this goal, the person [leader] who engages in reflection creates a sequence of ideas, projecting possible consequences that will result in a future outcome or series of events.[4]

Reflection, thus, can be a manner in which a person (school leader) has a conversation with herself or himself. To reflect, the person plays the role of both a player and an observer. This conversation is neither fleeting nor informal. To have such a conversation, both the player and the observer need to probe, analyze, examine, evaluate, apply, and integrate thoughts. And just as important, the conversation needs to address why this particular situation might be similar or different than previous situations, and to what extent.

Dewey submitted that the first stage of reflection is to experience "a state of doubt, hesitancy, perplexity, or mental difficulty."[5] Others have suggested that leaders must accept the turmoil found within the context of leadership, as such turmoil can help leaders frame current and future decision making in a more creative and empowering manner.

Arguably, the most influential scholar over the past century in this area has been Donald Schön. In his widely acclaimed book, *The Reflective Practitioner* (1983), Schön proposed the idea of reflective practices as the most critical component of a leader developing the knowledge and understanding to make sense of the ambiguities, conflicts, and dilemmas that face the leader on a regular basis. Schön then describes three concepts of such practice:

- *Knowing-in-Action*: This occurs when the leader responds to a situation in a manner that is instinctive and impromptu in nature. The leader, through experience, has learned how to respond to such situations in a rational and linear manner, which may include identification of the issue, analyzing options, and then making a decision without consuming many resources such as time and energy. According to Schön, leaders faced with these situations behave in a manner that is predictable and based upon some previous learning.

  However, Schön suggests that such actions are done in a spontaneous manner, and little, if any, thinking is required. Additionally, leaders are unaware of how and when they learned this skill, and further, they may not be able to describe the actual "knowing" that the process shows. Finally, Schön suggested that *knowing-in-action* might be the main difference between the leader who is proficient from those that are not.

- *Reflection-in-Action*: However, as leaders can attest, not all situations are predictable or constant. Surprises occur when unusual situations occur or when someone/something does not meet the leader's assumption and/or intentions. Schön contends that this occurs when the action is actually taking place, and that new, instantaneous responses may occur—learning to adjust while in the middle of the situation. Schön uses the example of a baseball pitcher who has made an adjustment, and as a result, "found the groove," leading to success. Another example Schön presents is that of jazz musicians who have "a feel" for their music in such a way that each of the members of the group can improvise according to the sounds they hear by listening to each other and developing an understanding of where the music is heading.

Accordingly, Schön submits that when a leader uses *reflection-in-action*, "he is not dependent on established theory and technique, but constructs a new theory unique to this case. Because his experimenting is a kind of action, implementation is built into his inquiry. We can still make a difference to the situation at hand—our thinking serves to reshape what we are doing while we are doing it" (68).

* *Reflection-on-Action*: This occurs when time is taken to think back on a particular experience in order to explore how *knowing-in-action* or *reflection-in-action* may have had an impact on the outcome of the experience, or perhaps, the leader may pause in the middle of an experience to contemplate.

Again, there is much more to this experience than just thinking about what has happened or what is happening. Reflection is more than pondering, and it is not something that can be done whenever time permits. On the contrary, reflection means wondering, questioning, debating, examining, and connecting. It is critical thinking from within. Not so much being critical in the sense that the leader did was right or wrong, but more in the sense of being analytical during or after a situation.

Reflective practice, thus, is the ability of a leader to develop a proficiency to make sense of the ambiguities and uncertainties of contemporary leadership. It is a way of *thinking*, not so much a way of *doing*. Simply put, there are many ways to *think about thinking* that can help the leader perceive and understand in a manner that may not be rational and segmented.

According to Kolb (1984), this represents experiential thinking and learning in a cycle of "adaptive learning models"—concrete experience, reflective observation, abstract conceptualization, and active experimentation. In terms of leadership, reflective practice is nested in participation and practice. Raelin and Coughlan submit,

> If a reflection opportunity is combined with work experience, they [the leader] can begin to realize the possibility of reframing experiences through reformulating "taken-for-granted" assumptions. Through such a reflective process, they [the leader] can use their lived experiences to generate practice learning and knowledge for action.[6]

THE STREETS OF LONDON

He was suffering by what is now known as writer's block. Having written a number of successful books and plays, the writer was struggling. He was worried about the pressure from the publisher to write more and write faster; he was concerned about his mounting debts; he was afraid that he and his family would end up living in the streets, as he had done as a young boy.

So nightly, he would walk the dark backstreets of London, sometimes covering as much as twenty miles in one evening, "many a night when all sober folks had gone to bed."[7] In the beginning, the walks were dominated by his worrying and self-pity. He was self-absorbed with his own success and oblivious to what was occurring around him on the streets of the city.

As a young man, Charles Dickens had been a freelance reporter, seeking out the daily drama and madness of London and its immediate environs. He spent much of this time thinking, writing, and sketching about the lives of politicians and the upper class, working for several magazines and news-papers, and traveling across Britain covering Parliament, election campaigns, and of course, the lives of the working class and the less fortunate. The writer also became quite adept at impersonating and mocking those with whom he interacted as a law clerk, as well as the upper-class merchants and factory owners for whom much of his passion would be aimed at throughout the rest of his life. And he began writing, becoming an accomplished writer by his thirtieth birthday.

His credits included novels such as *The Posthumous Papers of the Pickwick Club* (also known as *The Pickwick Papers* [1836]), *The Adventures of Oliver Twist* (1838), and *The Life and Adventures of Nicholas Nickleby* (1838). In addition, Dickens penned a number of short story collections (*Sketches by Boz*, 1836 and *The Mudfrog Papers*, 1837), plays (*The Village Coquettes*, 1836), and poetry (*The Fine Old Gentleman*, 1841). Dickens had become immensely popular in his home country of England, as well in Europe and America. From royalty to presidents, from publishing giants to university academics, he was in demand to speak, to lecture, to give advice. He traveled often and was paid handsomely.

Yet in spite of this success, by the early 1840s Dickens was struggling. He became distant to his wife and family, his friends and associates. He wasn't able to write. His only retreat was his nightly walks.

On these walks, he would reflect on his life, his success, and his struggles. Much of this time, Dickens would think back to his childhood, remembering when his family was frequently forced to move in and around London to keep the creditors away from his father, who was forever in debt. To help support the family, Charles—barely twelve years old—was hired to work in a factory pasting labels on pots of book blackening. For this he was paid six shillings per week for ten hours of work a day. The sensitive and lonely boy, who felt as if his family had "cast him to the streets," began to forge a lifelong curiosity into the bleak lives of the working poor, especially the young and vulnerable.

At some point, as the nightly walks continued, Dickens began to feel a revival in his spirit. Eventually, however, throughout the nights, he began to notice the young children scurrying to or from their jobs in the factories or bakeries. He began to follow the children to their homes—many times, finding that their homes were actually on the backstreets and alleys of London.

Other times, he would follow the children to where they worked. Dozens of children forced to do backbreaking work for meager sums of pay, often supervised by miserly and authoritative masters. He would try to talk with the children as they made their way home, and in the beginning, the children would often run away, thinking he was a thief. Eventually, he was able to gain their trust and listen to their stories. He tried to talk with the masters, but they would dismiss him or even threaten him.

The idea for a story finally emerged. He would write a story about the working children and the miserable lives they lived. He would satirize the factory owners as moneygrubbing curmudgeons. He would let the world know what was happening nightly in London. He began writing again with joy and clarity and creativity. He began to laugh more and worry less. He had found his voice again! The book, *A Christmas Carol*, was written by Charles Dickens. And with this book, Dickens introduced to the world the characters of Ebenezer Scrooge, the Cratchit Family (including Tiny Tim), and the Ghosts of Christmas Past, Present, and Yet to Come.

Charles Dickens had rediscovered his inner core, which was his source of purpose, his values, his visions, goals, and beliefs. His walks had provided an opportunity for him to become more introspective and self-aware, painful yet necessary.

In a scene toward the end of *A Christmas Carol*, Dickens illustrates the power of being rescued from this despair while being reconnected to one's inner core at the same time. Scrooge pleads with the Ghost for redemption and "to sponge away the writing on the stone."

> For the first time the hand appeared to shake. "Good spirit," he pursued, as down upon the ground he fell before it: "Your nature intercedes for me, and pities me. Assure me that I yet may change these shadows you have shown me, by an altered life!

TIME TO THINK

The Lake City School District (LCSD) had a student enrollment of almost fifteen thousand students attending its two high schools, four middle schools, and ten elementary schools. Typical of urban districts across the nation, more than two-thirds of the students in the LCSD were living in poverty and were struggling to meet academic standards set by the No Child Left Behind legislation of 2002.

Riverside High School is one of three high schools within the LCSD, with an enrollment of two thousand students. Over the past decade, RHS has restructured itself in a number of ways. It adopted the Smaller Learning

Community (SLC) concept seven years ago, in which the school was divided into four different houses. Students would be randomly selected to attend one of the houses over their entire four years at Riverside. The goal of this structure was to have students be supported academically and socially by a consistent team of teachers and staff in a smaller setting from within one of the four houses.

In addition, curriculum and instruction had been revamped. Much more time was spent on teaching across content areas, rather than teaching subjects in isolation. Block scheduling was implemented, and professional development surrounding increasing student engagement became a focus.

During the first few years of these initiatives, the data revealed some improvements. Graduation rates increased, as did attendance for each of the four houses. Dropout rates declined, and the number of students performing below standard on the state high school assessments declined as well. But year after year, despite improvements, RHS seemed to be always on the line between meeting and not meeting state standards. And with that always came the next "school improvement planning process" that was prescribed by the district administration.

> Dr. Thompson, something has to change! We—all of us—are at a breaking point. We are on a treadmill that is going nowhere fast! We just go-go-go all the time. File reports that go "who knows where?" put out fires every day, have meetings in which we are told what to do and are given little if any opportunity to think or talk or reflect about anything of substance. And we see you modeling this as well. You've lost that spark—that step in your walk—that everyone so appreciated when you got here ten years ago. That in spite of everything we face in our schools, that we—all of us—were going to make a difference. But something's missing and something needs to be done.

Dr. Paula Thompson did not expect this conversation when four of her best teachers asked to meet with her after school on a warm and sunny spring afternoon at the end of particular school day. During her ten years as principal of Riverside High School, Paula had intentionally cultivated a positive and transparent professional relationship with her best teachers. So as to not have such teachers perceived as "Paula's Pets," most of the interactions were on an informal basis. Sometimes, Paula would go visit one of these teachers during some free time and say, "I'm thinking of doing this, what do you think?" Sometimes the conversations would be while walking down the hall, in the parking lot, or over a cup of coffee.

Over time, this worked out so well that these teachers—most times individually, but sometimes in pairs or so—would often show up at Paula's office and engage in conversation regarding issues, concerns, and new ideas. Paula always found these conversation to be refreshing, candid, and stimulating, since she knew that these were her *superstars*—those teachers who the kids loved, who the parents wanted their children in these teachers' classes, and who had the respect of the rest of the faculty and were not only great people but great teachers as well!

Yet this was the first time that they all came at the same time and with such a message! Paula was surprised and taken aback at first. But true to her style, she listened more to what the group had to say.

Yet the more Paula listened to the teachers, the more she agreed with them. She, too, had felt that she "was moving nowhere fast" but thought maybe it was only her feeling this way—not her staff, particularly not her "superstars." One of the teachers shared the following with Paula:

> Just two weeks ago—when you completed a formal observation of me. Here, we are supposed to have a pre-observation conference, the actual observation itself, and then the post-observation conference. Do you remember what happened? The preconference took place in the hallway as you were leaving for a meeting; you only stayed for part of the class during the observation; and then you stopped by with the form for me to sign, stating that everything was excellent. And then, off you went to the next crisis.
>
> How do you think that made me feel? I know I am one of the best teachers here and you have always been so supportive. But really, what kind of feedback is that? I don't feel valued, you are not modeling the way, and it hurts!
>
> And if this is how we feel, just think about how other teachers must feel! And trust me, it rubs off on the students as well! But I'm afraid you are so busy doing everything that you do, that you are not seeing it—and it is right in front of you!

At the conclusion of the conversation, Paula thanked the group for their input and promised to do some "soul searching" over the weekend. She would get back to the group early next week with some thoughts and ideas. She also asked them to think of ideas and experiences that might help to get the discussion headed in a productive and positive fashion. After the teachers left, Paula closed the door to her office, sat back in her chair, and asked herself, "Now what?"

During the following weekend, Paula spent much time thinking about the meeting—what she heard, what she felt, and what she was going to do next. She researched, she read, she called old friends and mentors. Paula took several long walks. By Sunday night, she was as frustrated and concerned as she was at the beginning of the weekend. But she decided to contact the teachers, as she promised, and invited them to her house for dinner and discussion the following weekend. The only thing she requested was that they bring thoughts, ideas, questions, concerns, and everything else. In the meantime, Paula kept reaching out to colleagues and leaders—both in and outside of education—asking questions and seeking information.

The five teachers arrived at Paula's house about 1:00 Sunday afternoon. Paula had spent most of Saturday cooking and Sunday morning preparing for the meeting. She had several easels with newsprint situated throughout her family room. After exchanging pleasantries and small talk, Paula asked the group that, over the next several hours, she wanted to brainstorm and dig down to what these teachers were concerned about, what their perceptions were, and what they thought could and should be done. Paula promised them that she would listen and write, ask questions, and promised she would not be defensive. Anything and everything goes.

So for the next five hours, the group of six talked, shared, debated, laughed, cried, and even argued a bit. Paula, good to her promise, only spoke when she felt clarification was needed or when she felt another question needed to be asked. It was around six in the evening when Paula asked the group to summarize what was learned today. Among the comments were:

We are moving too fast and not stopping to think. Not only as an organization as a whole, but teachers and students as well.

We are all in urgent mode—everything is a crisis—we talk to each other, but not with each other.

We will never fulfill our mission if we continue to react, act, and move on.

We need to find time to think and share.

Faculty meetings and professional development have become nothing more than "sit and listen!"

Paula, you are modeling this and you have to change, and lead this change. And the five of us will work with you and support you. But you need to take the next steps.

During the next several weeks, Paula engaged a local university professor who had developed a scholarly agenda in the area of reflection and mindfulness. They met several times to discuss her concerns, and he gave her several publications to read. After reading these, she passed them along to her group of superstars, asking them to read and think about the contents. Within a week, each of the teachers came to Paula and indicated that she "was on to something."

At this point, the school year was ending, but the group decided to keep meeting throughout the summer, beginning with a session with the professor. As they discussed his work and those of others, the group was drawn to the concept of reflection, in which the professor shared the following:

Reflection is a conversation that you have with yourself. You are both the participant and the observer. You consider the context, and you give and receive attention.

Reflection is not just considering what happened and why, but to wonder, to probe, to connect. It is about why this event may be similar or different than others, and what does it matter. What am I learning? How will this help me? And then, imagine the power of an entire school thinking along these lines.

This reflective practice won't get rid of all the ills facing your school, but over time, people will be deeper thinkers, better thinkers, and perhaps, get folks to a place where learning is really cherished!

As the school year was coming to an end, Paula took some time to think about next steps. Her group of five teachers committed to working over the summer, but not in an "urgent-we-have-to-get-this-done-now" mode. As one of the teachers said, "I want time to read, think, share and reflect without being boxed in by time . . . plus, I want to enjoy my summer!"

Paula suggested that the group become engaged in a book study related to thinking and reflecting, particularly in the current educational context. Anna, a science teacher and department chair, suggested the book *The Mindful Leader* by Michael Carroll. She had read the book when it first came out in 2007 as part of a graduate course, and found it to be very engaging. She felt the book could be a first step of the learning process.

She shared with the group one of the most compelling lines from the author, who stated, "*The Mindful Leader* is about exploring the intimacy of sitting still and learning how such a simple act could transform our complicated and demanding workplace." Anna volunteered to be the study leader and to have meetings at her home every other Tuesday evening during the summer.

Everyone agreed; Paula ordered the books, and the first session was scheduled for three weeks after the school year ended. Paula was ecstatic, and as soon as the books arrived, she set out to read the entire book over the weekend. It was about halfway through the book that she realized that she was doing exactly what she shouldn't be doing: diving into the book, taking notes, and getting it done before everyone else! She stopped, put the book down, and walked away. Two days later, she picked up the book again, started over, and promised herself to (a) read no more than ten pages at a sitting; (b) think deeply about what she had just read; (c) only write down questions that she wanted to share with others. And she vowed to be "one of the group, not the boss."

The group met five times over the summer, and though the first session started slowly, Anna did a wonderful job of facilitating the sessions, while everyone else—including Paula—became deeply engaged in the discussion of the book, as well as the potential impact it could have on both the staff and students at RHS. At each subsequent session, members would bring articles and resources to share. Andre, a long-time social studies teacher, brought materials related to "reflective practice for educators," proposing that this might be a place to start with the faculty.

By the end of the last session, the group agreed to use the mindfulness and reflective practice model. Paula indicated that she would "find" professional development funds and begin the formal process as early as January of the upcoming school year.

It was also agreed that each of the five teachers would informally engage three other teachers in book studies during the fall semester, similar to what occurred during the summer. However, no official announcement would be made of this.

Paula and the group agreed that for the fall semester, a portion of each faculty meeting (twice per month after school on Mondays) would be discussion around the topic of reflection in a way that would not be perceived as "just another thing on the plates of teachers," nor in a way that could be perceived as the next "idea du jour/mandate."

During the first three months of the new school year, the informal book studies occurred, and in a steady manner, Paula and the group of five (now calling themselves "The Reflectors") engaged faculty in deliberate discussions regarding the issue of how to "slow down, think, reflect, and move on." Articles, videos, and simulations were presented at faculty meetings, with the rule of thumb being "30 minutes max—let's not overwhelm anyone." Naturally, some of the faculty enjoyed these experiences, some were ambivalent, and others were somewhat negative.

Paula was able to send two of "The Reflectors" to a conference in Chicago, titled "Educators Learning and Modeling from Experience through Reflection." At this conference, they were not only able to experience what others in education were doing to address reflective practice in their schools but also saw examples of formal professional development programs for faculties to experience as a whole.

As the second semester began, the group made contact with a school from a nearby state that had developed and implemented a formal program of reflective thinking in terms of both faculty and students. At this school, curriculum, instruction, and assessments were each revised in a manner that allowed for reflective practice to occur on a regular and consistent basis. The team selected five other teachers from RHS to visit the school and report back. In addition, the principals and department chairs from the school in the nearby state were invited to spend an entire professional development day with the RHS faculty and staff during the spring.

During the next year, Paula and the team decided to move slowly and surely with the concept. Teachers were encouraged to integrate reflective practice with not only their teaching but with all aspects of life at RHS. Conflict resolution, problem solving, relations among staff and students were but a few of the areas in which this concept was applied. Teachers were asked to share their lessons and experiences with reflective practice in a manner that was not evaluative, but in a way that helped everyone to grow.

Three years later, Paula was asked to reflect upon what had occurred at RHS. She stated,

> Two things have improved for the better at our school. First, I am a much better leader now than before. Yes, my plate is full and it seems we keep getting more and more mandates. But even with that, I really have begun to take time to think about things that are happening—what has happened, why it happened, what I/we did, what did we learn from this.
>
> So really, I'm not running around trying to solve everyone's problems—including my own—and then jumping into the next issue. No, I am much more deliberate and thoughtful about everything. And I am very conscientious about modeling this reflective thinking with everyone I deal with—staff, students, parents, and the greater community.
>
> The second thing that has improved has been the overall culture of the school. Both staff and students, I feel, are much more deliberate in their thinking and interactions, as they constantly are asked to or request others to be a reflective practitioner. For three years now, we have given a survey to teachers and students regarding the culture and climate of the school, and each year the results show that both groups see the culture of the school to be positive and less hurried.
>
> So, at the end of the day, I'm better, the school is better, and we are all much better at thinking and reflecting!

LEARNING FOR LEADING

We had the experience but missed the meaning.
And approach to the meaning restores the experience in a different form. [8]
—T. S. Eliot

Follow around any school leader—superintendent or principal—for a week or so, and one could probably make the following conclusions: the life of the school leader is full of chaos, ambiguity, and surprises. Many times, the leader is dealing with unhappy people—particularly adults—who can't or won't listen to reason. Or, the leader is constantly "putting out fires" that may or may not be urgent or important at that particular time. Thus, chaos sets in when the many different issues appear at almost the same time, as if the whole organization wants and needs an answer immediately from the leader, and the answer needs to be the one they want! If not, chaos continues and grows!

Ambiguity sets in when the school leader tries to resolve such issues but is uncertain how to act (decide). The leader may ask herself or himself, "Do I resolve this the same way I did before?" "To what extent do I involve others?" "What if I don't have an answer at the moment people are demanding one?"

And finally, there are the surprises that the school leader is not expecting. A superintendent finds out that the majority of the board that was responsible for hiring her or him has been voted out of office. Or the school principal learns that her or his best teacher has decided to transfer to another school!

In addition, now more than ever, school leaders are faced with more accountability, more mandates, and less support than ever. It seems that more and more is being expected, all within the same amount of time. School leadership, for many, is becoming more of doing and much less of thinking. Thus, it would behoove all school leaders to consider becoming a reflective leader—more of a thinker, and less of a doer. This is exactly opposite of what those outside the leader's office want. But it is exactly what is needed. It won't be easy, and it won't happen overnight.

Margaret Wheatley stated,

> In this culture of overreaction and constant judgment, it takes great discipline to refrain from creating made-in-the-moment dramas. Everyone else is, so why shouldn't we? Our only defense against this seduction is to be mindful, skilled at watching our reactions as quickly as possible. If we can notice that we're caught up in emotions, then we stop our story lines from blossoming into full-blown dramatic operas. Pausing before we react is so powerful because it gives us time to quiet the mind. And once we do, we discover that gentleness, decency and bravery are available.[9]

And so, how does a school leader—in the face of this constant and ever-increasing tension—become more of a thinker, more reflective, more mindful? First of all, it won't be easy, and it can't be done overnight. For example, many of us have at one time or another probably tried to lose weight. Eat less and exercise more. But those who stick to the plan will most likely begin to see results, which can be measured by a scale and a tape measure (for around the middle!). But even for those who commit to this, doing it alone is not as likely to produce results over the long term as when done in concert with others. Having support and giving support is critical to success.

Yet changing a habit of mind can often be daunting, since there are really no scales or measuring tapes available. Even the thought of "thinking about thinking" can cause many different reactions, with most being negative ("I don't have time to think!"). But many school leaders have, in fact, become more reflective and actually do think about thinking. And just like Paula in the story, most if not all feel much better about themselves, about their leadership, and about those for whom they lead.

And so, the following list is offered to those school leaders who are considering a change from being the proverbial "doer" to more of a "think-er." The list has been gathered over the past two decades, from formal research projects to anecdotal conversations with superintendents and school principals, regardless of gender, ethnicity, age, experience, or location. As the Chinese philosopher Lao-tzu said more than two thousand years ago, "A journey of a thousand miles begins with a single step."

- As simple as it sounds, the sooner the school leader begins to "think about thinking," the better. Again, this is easier said than done, and starting this with someone else might be very helpful. Either way, the leader must start! Whether it's jogging, relaxing on the porch, driving to work, driving home from work, or just hanging out at the beach, "thinking about thinking" can start a process by which the school leader can help to link learning to job performance. In its simplest terms, reflective thinking can be addressing questions such as: What happened? Why did it happen? Who was involved? How did I react? and if it happened again, What would I do differently (if anything)?
- A more formal approach to reflective thinking is to be both the "actor" and the "critic." When thinking about a particular event, the school leader first does a self-analysis of the event, placing herself or himself squarely in focus (similar to the questions above). However, once this is completed, the leader then becomes a critic, moving away from self to a more judgmental position in which a complete analysis occurs. A much deeper analysis of the event(s) can almost certainly occur. Following this step, the leader then begins to prepare for future events through creative and innovative ways to deal with such events, based upon this reflective thinking.
- At some point, the issue of whether to reflect alone or with someone else will likely surface. In the beginning, the leader may want to keep such thoughts to herself or himself, considering the nature of the issues being contemplated as well as the fear of being looked at as being a weak leader. Nonetheless, school leaders generally understand the power of being part of a team, in which collaboration and deep discussions occur, often culminating with richer feedback, thoughts, and a deeper sense of self, than one could on their own.
- One of the greatest strengths that most, if not all, school leaders have is that of looking out for others. Whether it's students, faculty, staff, or members of the community, school leaders often take on the responsibilities and welfare of others. And while this is admirable, it is often at the cost of the leader's own being. Stephen Covey suggested that the only way for a person to continuously grow is to "sharpen the saw," in which one's own resources, energy, and health are balanced and renewed through both formal and informal physical, emotional, spiritual, and social exercises. The use of reflective thinking can certainly be attached to each of these exercises.

Wheatley suggests the following as a possible "first step" of the reflective thinking process, which she learned from a Tibetan monk:

Each morning he chooses one behavior or quality he will focus on that day. Perhaps today he'll seek opportunities to practice forgiveness, or to be less reactive when provoked, or to be a better listener. At the close of the day, just before sleep, he reflects on how he did. He is quick to emphasize that this self-assessment is not to blame or punish himself with guilt and remorse for what he failed to do well. Quite the opposite. He ends his reflection with expressions of gratitude and happiness directed toward himself. If doesn't matter whether he messed up—he is delighted and grateful that he is working to develop these qualities himself.[10]

Thus, reflective thinking and practice can help the school leader develop a better sense of self-awareness, something that is often secondary to the harried pace of leading schools in the contemporary context. Self-awareness cultivates other leadership qualities necessary for success. And in order to become more self-aware, the leader needs to "think about thinking" first, and then through various mental exercises—whether alone or with others—practice thinking and reflecting upon events, so that none of the meanings from the many different and unusual events will not be missed.

Chapter Five

Surviving and Thriving

There is evidence that four women played a substantial role in the education of Eleanor Roosevelt, tutoring her in politics, strategy, and public policy, encouraging her to open up emotionally, building her sense of confidence and self-esteem. When Eleanor first came into contact with these bold and successful women, she found herself in awe of the professional status they had acquired. "If I had to go out and earn my own living," she conceded, "I doubt if I'd even make a very good cleaning woman."

In the space of two years, and with the guidance of her female colleagues, Eleanor emerged as a major force in New York public life. For Sara [Eleanor's mother-in-law, FDR's mother], Eleanor's transformation was harder to accept. Sara was appalled at the idea of a well-bred woman spending so much time away from home in the public eye. A woman's place was with her husband and her children. "My generation did not do those things," Sarah explained. [1]

In 1838, Buffalo, New York, had the distinction of appointing the first superintendent of schools in the United States, Mr. Oliver G. Steele. Since then, the Buffalo School District has had almost forty school superintendents. In 2015, Buffalo hired its eighth superintendent *since* 2000, which averages out to less than two years per superintendent over this time period!

Yet Buffalo is not unique in having such a high rate of turnover for its school superintendents during the first two decades of the twenty-first century. Consider the following:

- Of the 133 school districts within the state of Virginia, more than one-half of the superintendents turned over between 2012 and 2014.
- In California, 45 percent of all school districts have had superintendent turnover from 2006 to 2009, including 71 percent of all large school districts.

- Between 2009 and 2011, more than 30 percent of the school superintendents left their positions in New Jersey.
- Kansas City, Missouri, had twenty-five superintendents over a forty-year period, between 1983 and 2008.
- In 2008, St. Louis hired their eighth superintendent in five years.
- Since 2000, the city of Baltimore has had six superintendents.

It is a familiar story. The board of education hires an energetic and charismatic new leader to replace the previous superintendent who left (retired, resigned, quit, fired, and left for another district). The excitement of having this new leader abounds throughout the district. The honeymoon lasts somewhere between six and eighteen months.

Sooner or later, things begin to change. Relationships go sour. The leader may clash with the teachers' union or make a decision that upsets a particular constituent group within the district. A board election brings on new members, who had nothing to do with the selection of this superintendent. These board members may have selected agendas that got them elected, and since they may not have any allegiance to the superintendent, the inevitable clashes occur. And before one realizes, the superintendent has left this district and gone elsewhere.

The literature abounds with numerous examples of what was described above. Sometimes, even when the superintendent has provided positive leadership with reforms and results the board was seeking, public pressure, tension, and the politics found within the contemporary context of school leadership will result in the superintendent leaving early. The list of high-profile school districts that recruited reform-minded superintendents who leave before their contract is up continues to grow, including Baltimore, Buffalo, Chicago, Kansas City, Miami-Dade, Philadelphia, San Francisco, and St. Louis, to name just a few.

As of 2014, the average tenure of superintendents within the Council of Great City Schools was 3.18 years, up from 2.80 years in 2003, but down from 3.64 years in 2010.[2]

WHY SO MUCH TURNOVER?

During the past several decades, much has been written about superintendent turnover as well as if there is a real or perceived shortage of superintendents. Regarding the latter, some feel that there is such a shortage, based upon the decrease in the number of applicants, and in some cases, the lack of quality applicants for the position. However, as we shall see in the next section, there appears to be a whole new supply of applicants ready, willing, and able to serve as superintendents.

As for the actual turnover of superintendents across the country, one of the main reasons is that the "baby boom" generation is at the point of retiring in record numbers. One only needs to read newspapers and educational magazines to see the shortage of teachers, principals, and superintendents in many areas across the country. Additionally, according to the American Association of School Administrators (AASA), a 2010 national survey found the top four reasons for superintendents to leave their previous superintendency were:

1. Assume a new challenge (30.3 percent)
2. School board conflict (15.3 percent)
3. To supplement a pension (13.7 percent)
4. Seek a higher-performing school district (11.4 percent)[3]

In addition to this list, there are other related reasons for the amount of turnover.

• *Hired to be fired*: an old adage in major league baseball is that when a team hires a new manager, it is only a matter of time before the manager will get fired. And since there are only thirty teams in major league baseball, a fired manager has very limited options. Superintendents, however, do have more options if they do get fired or are forced out. For example, New York State has close to eight hundred school districts, each having a superintendent of schools. But it is rare to see a superintendent be the leader of a particular school district for more than a decade, which was more of the norm than the exception several decades ago. As one superintendent said,

> Too many things can and will change that I have no control over. I try to negotiate a five-year contract. Then, during those five years, I think I can get a number of things accomplished. If I can last through my contract, I will be a very happy person. But I also know that if the board wants to get rid of me, they can and will. Social media has driven even the most minute issue to the "front page" of Internet sites.
>
> Can you imagine a major corporation having a new CEO every three to five years? I think the days of staying in one district for an entire career—from teacher to principal to central office and finally the superintendency—are for the most part over. There really seems to be a culture of "what have you done for us lately?" and if there is a perception that it is not enough, well, it's only a matter of time.

• *Dysfunctional school boards*: school boards, for the most part, are political entities. Some boards are selected; others are elected. Regardless of the size of the school district, location of the school district, or the demographics of the school district, there is a tendency on the part of many boards across the nation to micromanage.

Few boards have long-term strategic plans, and those who do have such plans may want to change such at a moment's notice. Priorities can change as elections occur, and a shift in the balance of power on the board can occur as well, leaving the superintendent in the middle. It doesn't take much to have such a shift, especially on a smaller board—such as a five-person board—when a new member or two comes onto the board. One superintendent shared the following:

> So, I was voted in 8–1 as the new superintendent in early May. I took over on July 1, and by August 1, two of the board members who had voted in favor of me left the board. Then two more left the board by the end of September (both of these board members told the local press that "we have the right person as superintendent, we don't need to stay on anymore"). The board wanted to hold a special election to replace the four departed members, but decided not to in order to save money, instead using an obscure state education law that allows the board to select new members for terms that equate to the original member's term.
>
> Applications were accepted for interviews, and guess what? Four people signed up! Within two weeks, these new board members were seated, and they had no allegiance to me as the new superintendent and each had their own agenda. By the end of the calendar year, executive sessions had turned into shouting matches among board members, leaking of confidential information occurred from the meetings, and I was being pulled in every direction. It was a disaster! Talk about a short honeymoon! I got out as soon as I could! And I am glad I did. In the last five years, that district has gone through three more superintendents!

• *Grass is greener on the other side*: salaries for superintendents have increased dramatically over the past two decades in most sections of the country. Six-figure salaries are the norm, not the exception, and many superintendents are very willing to move to other districts where the compensation is considerably higher. Some superintendents, for example, move from rural areas, where the pay is less, to more affluent suburban areas, and as long as they stay within the state, they will continue to have their retirement benefits increase at the newer and higher salary. Consider what the following superintendent did:

> I was closing in on thirty-five years and thinking of retiring—I pretty much maxed out on my retirement benefits. I would have a nice retirement to live on, but I wanted to work maybe five years or more. Within driving distance of where I was presently employed was another state, where they paid superintendents much more than where I was.
>
> So I applied for superintendency in that state and was offered a position at a substantially higher salary. I retired in my "home" state and began collecting my retirement there, and at the same time, began working as a superintendent in the other state. It has turned out to be a financial boom for me.

• *It's too political*: Tip O'Neill, the one-time Speaker of the House of Representatives, once said that "all politics is local." And none more so than for the contemporary school superintendent. From teacher unions to parent groups to split school boards, the superintendent must constantly juggle many political balls in the air. Regardless if one is the superintendent of a small school district (where everyone knows your name, where you live, where you shop) or that of a large school district (after the mayor, the superintendent may be the most recognized person), the political nature of the job can be overwhelming, and to the unprepared, intimidating and very stressful. As one superintendent said,

> I never knew what the political nature of the job was until I actually became the superintendent and sat in on the school board's executive session. All protocol went out the window, and pretty much I was told who to work with, who not to work with, who to stay away from, and who to hire or not hire. And of course, there were times when the board members disagreed among themselves as to who I should work with.
>
> One time, during tense negotiations with the teachers' union, some of the members told me to walk away from the negotiations, some told me to keep negotiating, and the rest just sat silent. Parents were after me to reach a settlement so their kids would not be affected by this; the taxpayers in the community (nonparents) wanted me to hold the line and "keep the teachers in line," and every morning for a month, a group of teachers would protest in front on my house—chanting and holding signs—even on the weekends!

• *Is it really about student achievement?* Perhaps there has never been a time in the history of education in the United States when there has been more discourse, debate, and policy regarding public schools. Since the implementation of the No Child Left Behind legislation in 2002, states, school districts, and individual schools have been under the microscope in terms of ensuring that student achievement improves and that all educational entities will be held accountable. The measuring stick for success has been the ever-increasing use of standardized testing in elementary and secondary schools. And since the bottom line of standardized tests is the score, states, districts, and schools are often ranked from top to bottom within a jurisdiction.

The person most likely to be held accountable for this at the school level is the principal, and at the district level it is the superintendent. One critic of educational policy stated, "If you can tell me the zip code of where a student goes to school, I can tell you if test scores at that school (district) are high or not!" To many superintendents, the message is strong and clear: *Just get those test scores up!*

And so, against their own principles of how students learn and what great instruction really is, many superintendents—particularly in high poverty areas where test scores are likely to be lower and/or not improving—are pressured into having instruction staff "teach to the test," and to create schedules in which the arts and physical education are cut back or even eliminated in order to have students receive more instructional time in the "tested" areas, oftentimes with the instruction being scripted and programmed curriculum. Many school leaders have become frustrated with the standardized testing results being the only measurement the public and the board will use. Here is what one former superintendent said:

> I had been in education for more than three decades and I was a darn good English teacher. I knew that before I could teach the kids any of the content, I first had to build relationships. And I did. And when I became principal of a school that became my mantra. But over the last decade, as I moved up the ladder through central office and eventually the superintendency, it became evident to me that relationships were secondary.
>
> Test scores were primary. So, I had to be the instructional leader of the district and hold principals and teachers accountable for what an eight-year-old does on a standardized test the third Tuesday of March. And of course, the board held me accountable as well. When I realized that I was becoming another promoter of "test score mania," that's when I got out.

HELP WANTED: WHO WANTS THIS JOB?

After reading the previous section, one might conclude that (a) no one in their right mind would want to be a superintendent, and (b) there must be a shortage of candidates considering the turnover and strife that seems to go hand in hand with the job. In short, the answer to (a) is that there are plenty of well-educated, sane people who like being the superintendent and would like to become a superintendent.

Furthermore, as we shall see, there is a group in the field of education whose numbers are increasing dramatically in terms of becoming school superintendents. And depending on who you listen to or read, a shortage of superintendents may or may not exist. The research is not clear on either the quantitative or qualitative figures that may or may not support the notion of a shortage. It just is not clear at this point.

In fact, according to AASA, a national survey of superintendents found the following:

- More than 69 percent of current superintendents were *very satisfied* with their career choice as a superintendent, and more than 27 percent indicated they were *moderately satisfied.*
- When asked if they would follow the same career path given an opportunity to retrace their steps, more than 63 percent said they *definitely* would choose this path again, while an additional 25 percent indicated they *probably* would choose the same path again.

What is known, though, is that there are a number of reasons why educators continue to get into the superintendent pipeline.

- *Salary and Benefits*: across the United States, it is no longer uncommon for superintendents to have starting salaries over the $100,000 mark. In addition, many of the large urban districts and wealthier suburban districts, particularly in the East and Midwest, are paying superintendents over $200,000 for salary, in addition to benefits! And if one considers that many of these aspiring superintendents began as teachers two or three decades ago making $20,000 a year, such salaries, along with the benefits (particularly health and pension), can be very enticing.
- *Difference Makers*: there have always been and probably always will (we hope!) those who want to be a superintendent in order to make a difference on a larger scale. These are educators who have been very successful in the classroom, in school-level administration, and in the central office as well. Because of such success, these educators want to be the school district leader in order to make a difference across the entire district.
- *The Challenge*: this group looks at the position of superintendent as a challenge to change the status quo, particularly in school districts that have had low student achievement in the past, political strife, and perhaps constant turnover of school leaders. This group looks past the issues that the district may have, and really believes that their style, experience, and characteristics can overcome such issues, if only given the chance.

FACES IN THE CROWD: THE MORE THINGS CHANGE, THE MORE THEY REMAIN THE SAME

Perhaps the most significant change in the makeup of the American school superintendency over that past two decades has been the increasing number of female superintendents. As shown below, the percentage of superintendents who are female has increased almost sixfold from 1990 to 2010.

At face value, it appears that women are making significant inroads into the superintendency, particularly after almost a century of being excluded. Women, in fact, are not a minority of the general population; in fact, they are a slight majority. In addition, for most of the twentieth century and continuing into the twenty-first century, female teachers have been an overwhelming majority in terms of gender, consistently falling somewhere between 70 percent and 80 percent of the total teachers in the United States. For example, in the 2011 to 2012 school year, more than 76 percent of teachers in public schools were female, including 89 percent in elementary schools and 58 percent in high schools.[4]

Table 5.1.   Percentage of Superintendents Who Are Female*

Year	Percent
1910	8.9%
1930	11.0%
1950	9.0%
1970	3.4%
1990	4.9%
2000	13.7%
2010	24.1%

Throughout the history of American education—as in other industries—men have been perceived as being more suitable than women for positions of leadership. Traditional gender stereotypes regarding leadership are a major reason for such perceptions, which have ultimately left women out of the superintendency. In the case of education, male leaders are supposed to be the disciplinarian, the task master, more assertive, and have a better grasp of such issues as budgets, facilities, negotiations, and strategic planning. On the other hand, female educational leaders are supposed to be nurturing, the curriculum and instructional expert, and the relationship builder.

Females have faced, and continue to face, barriers and challenges to the superintendency. There has been much research completed over the past several decades that provides a list of such barriers, in spite of the fact that there has been much federal and state legislation outlawing discrimination on the basis of gender.

For example, Polka and Litchka (2008) found that female superintendents in Georgia and New York were more likely to face a crisis in their professional and personal life while being the superintendent of schools. Litchka, Fenzel, and Polka (2010) found that female superintendents faced higher levels of stress than their male counterparts did, and coped with stress less effectively as well.

Well into the twentieth century, current and aspiring female superintendents are still facing barriers that males generally do not face, substantiated within the contemporary research context:

- *Glass Ceiling*: for many females who aspire to become the superintendent of schools, they may be considered for a position of assistant superintendent (particularly for curriculum and instruction) but never for the top job (Katz 2004).

- *Glass Windows*: as mentioned above, once a female becomes a superintendent, she may be steered exclusively toward the curriculum and instruction side of the district and away from the business and management side.
- *Gatekeeper Discrimination*: search firms may typecast ("pigeonhole") female candidates toward smaller and "safer" school districts (Glass, Bjork, and Brunner 2006).
- *Different Expectations*: in spite of credentials and experiences similar to males, women aspiring to be the superintendent may decide against it, since women tend to have more responsibilities for the home and family, and ultimately, the personal cost would be too high (Dana and Bourisaw 2006).
- *Role Theory*: female leaders, including superintendents, are perceived in terms of how they are expected by society to behave, what they are supposed to do (and not do), and subsequently how they behave (Brunner and Grogan 2007).
- *Physical Appearance*: if the female candidate for the superintendency looks "too good" and is "too pretty," then she can't be very smart or strong enough for this position.
- *Women School Board Members*: female candidates are seen in a competitive light and as a threat to female school board members or other females in school district leadership positions.

As McGee-Banks suggests,

> The assumption that leadership requires male characteristics has led to a body of research in which women and people of color are compared to White men. This research results in men being held up as the ideal to which women and people of color are compared. Conceptualizing research on leaders as a mirror in which women and people of color are expected to be a reflection of White men ultimately marginalizes these two groups because they are viewed as having fewer skills and less power. [5]

In addition to these barriers, once a female is selected as the superintendent, she will likely face a leadership paradox based solely on gender stereotyping: if she displays the traditional qualities of female leadership listed above, she may not be taken as seriously as her male counterpart, or be relegated to only dealing with "curriculum stuff" and other softer issues. On the other hand, if she displays a more stereotypical male leadership—being assertive, controlling, domineering, and aggressive—especially in areas that are usually left with the "good old boys," most likely she will be viewed in a much more negative manner.

And as we shall see later in the chapter, the female superintendent can be treated in a most cruel and unprofessional manner. Thus, in terms of effective leadership for school superintendents, female leaders are more likely to be viewed differently and more negatively than male leaders who may exhibit the exact same behaviors!

A SEAT AT THE TABLE

> There is a type of woman who cannot remain at home. . . . In spite of the place where her children and her family take up in her life, her nature and being demand something more; she cannot divorce herself from a larger social life. She cannot let her children narrow her horizon. And for such a woman, there is no rest.
> —Golda Meir[6]

The last decade of the nineteenth century was not particularly kind to the Mabovitch family, who resided in the Ukrainian city of Kiev. Of the six children born to the father, Moshe, and the mother, Bluma, only two sisters, Sheyna and Goldie, would survive childhood and live to see the twentieth century. The family lived in abject poverty as the father, a cabinetmaker, could only find enough work for the family to barely survive upon.

The Mabovitch family was also Jewish, and during this time, perhaps no city in Russia was more anti-Semitic than Kiev. Jews in Russia had been tormented for many decades, particularly during the last half of the nineteenth century, since Catherine the Great, who referred to Jews as "evil influences," made it official policy that Russian Jews were to be confined to the Pale of Settlement in Eastern Europe.

This was a region of Imperial Russia in which permanent residency by Jews was allowed and beyond which Jewish permanent residency was generally prohibited. This area, which included pieces of Russian Poland, parts of the Ukraine, Lithuania, Belorussia, the Crimea, and Bessarabia, was considered to be the farthest reaches of the empire and least economically significant. By the turn of the century, more than 90 percent of Russian Jews were legally confined to the Pale of Settlement.

It was in 1903 that Moshe Yitzhak Mabovitch, one of more than almost eighty thousand Jews from Eastern Europe, left Russia for America, arriving in New York and eventually settling in Milwaukee, Wisconsin. Goldie, Sheyna, and their mother, Bluma, would immigrate to the United States in 1906, rejoining Moshe, who had a job as a railroad carpenter. Within a week of arriving and speaking little if any English, Bluma opened a grocery store.

Against the wishes of her parents—who thought that "men don't like smart girls" and "girls don't need an education; they need to be prepared for marriage"—Goldie wanted to go to school and become a teacher. She became an excellent student, always at or near the top of her class. It was during this time period that Goldie became very involved in fund-raising for needy students, organizing book and food drives, and even led a demonstration against the anti-Semitism she had experienced at her school. In 1912, at the age of fourteen, she left home to join Sheyna in Denver.

Though she would return to Milwaukee and finish high school, Golda (no longer Goldie) threw herself into social causes in both Milwaukee and Chicago, and by 1917, she married Morris Meyerson, who she met in Denver. Within a year, she coaxed Morris into moving to Palestine to join a collective farm and help the fight for Jewish independence.

Over the next four decades, Golda Meir would rise in Israeli politics, as she would play a critical role in Israel's struggle for independence, the establishment of Israel as a state, and its struggle for survival in a region surrounded by enemy Arab nations. In 1946, Golda became head of the political department of the Jewish Agency, which represented the Jewish refugees who had fled Europe in violation of British immigration regulations.

In 1948, she was one of twenty-four signatories of Israel's Proclamation of Independence. Golda was elected to the first-ever Knesset, the Israeli parliament, and then would serve as an ambassador to the Soviet Union (1948–1949), minister of Foreign Affairs (1956–1966), and prime minister of Israel (1969–1974). Three principles would guide Golda through her career: (1) Jews are always the underdog; (2) true democracy can only occur through socialism; (3) as a woman, she would do everything possible and more to get a seat at the table of power dominated by men (a "reluctant feminist," as she was once called).

While her years as prime minister would bring her to the world stage as the first woman leader of a Western nation, perhaps Golda's finest moment of support for Israel's survival occurred in 1948, when Israel, having just declared its independence, was beset with financial problems and the threat of invasion by neighboring Arab states.

In January 1948, the Jewish Agency determined that the fledgling country would need more than $175 million to win and sustain their war for independence. The treasurer thought, at the time, that someone of importance, such as David Ben-Gurion, could go to the United States and raise between $7 and $8 million for the war effort. As Arab armies were poised for attack, it was decided, however, the Ben-Gurion would remain in Palestine, and that Golda Meir would go to America in search of funds. The treasurer told her that if she could raise $10 million, it would exceed all expectations.

Golda Meir landed in New York City on January 23, 1948, in a blinding snowstorm, met only by her son, Menachem. She would spend the next seven weeks in a flurry of speeches and fund-raising activities within the United States. While some of the leaders of the various major American Jewish organizations were not overly enthusiastic to listen to the "little lady from Palestine" asking for yet more donations, Golda did discover a new generation of American Jews who were, in fact, very willing to listen and donate.

These American Jews—many who had come to America and become very wealthy and successful—were deeply affected and influenced by what had happened to them, their families, and other Jews in Europe over the past three decades. To many of these American Jews, they felt angry and guilty and wanted to be a part of what was about to happen in Palestine. Golda would tap into this energy over the next seven weeks.

Originally, Golda tried to get on the agenda of the General Assembly of the Council of Jewish Federations, which was meeting in Chicago in late January 1948. However, the matter of Palestine was not on the agenda, and it was only through perseverance and political maneuvering that she was given a slot on the agenda. She was told, however, to keep her speech short, get right to the point, don't be emotional, don't make demands, and don't take more than five minutes. The audience was most skeptical.

For her speech she wore a simple black dress, wore no jewelry or make-up, and had her hair pulled back tightly in a bun. For the next thirty-five minutes (!), she energized and galvanized the large audience. Speaking quietly and using no notes, she asked for $25 million in donations! Golda implored the audience that Jews around the world, particularly in the United States, must unify in support of the impending war for independence. In her speech, she declared:

> We shall fight in the Negev, and fight in the Galil and will fight on the outskirts of Jerusalem until the very end . . . The Jewish community of Palestine will raise no white flag. The decision is taken; nobody can change it. You can only decide one thing: whether we shall be victorious in this fight or whether the Mufti will be victorious. That decision American Jews can make. It has to be made quickly, within hours, within days. I beg of you—don't be too late. Don't be bitterly sorry three months from now for what you failed to do today. The time is now. [7]

The speech had an immediate impact. Donations began to pour in immediately, the American press took note, and Golda Meir was being invited to speak all across America. She spoke in Omaha, Tulsa, Houston, Dallas, Los Angeles, Cleveland, Miami, and New York. By February 3, she notified Ben-Gurion that she had raised $15 million, including $5 million in one day in Miami! By then end of February, the figure was at $30 million, and by the time she arrived back in Jerusalem in March, Golda Meir had raised more than $50 million! As Ben-Gurion would write

> Someday, when history will be written, it will be said that there was a Jewish woman who got the money which made the state possible. And that woman was Golda Meir. [8]

As powerful and influential as she would become both in Israel and on the world stage, Golda Meir was held back to a certain degree by the overall attitude toward women in politics. Ben-Gurion once referred to her as the "only man in the Cabinet" (later, she once stated, "I very much doubt that any man in the cabinet would have been flattered if I had said about him that he was the only woman in the government!").[9]

She once lost a very close election for mayor of Jerusalem due to influential conservative Jews who withheld support because they felt a woman should not be allowed to be in such a position. And on a number of occasions, she was both publicly and privately criticized for not speaking in a more feminine manner. Once, after giving a speech in New York City, the president of a local chapter of a Jewish organization said to her:

> Look Golda . . . you speak very well but you don't speak like a woman. When other women speak to us, they cry and we cry. But you talk like a man, so no one can cry.[10]

On March 17, 1969, Golda was elected as the prime minister of Israel, the first woman to hold that office in the history of the country and only the fourth woman in the world to hold such an office. Fresh off the stunning victory in the 1967 Six-Day War, Israel had taken on an aura of invincibility, both politically and militarily. During this time, the government never expected Arab states to plan another attack against their homeland—at least not in the foreseeable future. Much of the attention would be paid on the international scene where terrorist attacks against Israel were increasing. One such example was the massacre of Israeli athletes at the Munich Olympics in 1972.

In the summer of 1973, Meir received news that Syrian forces were beginning to form on the Golan Heights. Upset by such news, Meir thought this was eerily similar to what had happened in 1967. Despite the fact that the Knesset passed a resolution granting Meir the power to have a full-scale deployment of the military, her advisor, Minister of Defense Moshe Dayan, the hero of the Six-Day War, vehemently opposed her. On October 5, Meir and Dayan met. According to those close to the situation, Dayan did not think that "she" was capable of making such decisions and it should be left to those with military background and experience. Six hours after this meeting, war broke out between Syria and Israel.

Although Israel would initially be shaken by these hostilities, eventually they prevailed. However, Golda Meir received much criticism for her lack of making a decision when she had all of the information that the attack was imminent. She would remain in office until June 3, 1974, when she resigned.

SHATTERING THE GLASS

Penny Edwards grew up in a very competitive environment. There were five children in her family, and she was the only girl. Two brothers were older—the oldest by three years—and two brothers were younger—the youngest by four years. They lived less than a block from the city park, where there were baseball fields, a basketball court, a tennis court, an outdoor ice skating rink, and an open field that was used by the neighborhood kids for all kinds of sports activities (depending on the season): football, soccer, and even a golf range! During the summer, the weekends, and after school, you could always find Penny, her brothers, and the neighborhood kids at the park.

But the competitive spirit of the Edwards children did not just happen by chance. Their father, Dean Edwards, was a physical education teacher, athletic director, football coach, basketball coach, and tennis coach at the local high school. He was very competitive and successful as well, and would eventually be elected to three different halls of fame for his success as both a coach and athletic director. To his own children, his players, and those coaches who worked for him at the high school, athletic competition was the best way to learn and grow as a person, and his dictum to all was: play by the rules, play harder than the others, play all the sports, and winning is really important but be a good sport!

Mary Edwards, the wife of Dean and mother of the five Edwards children, was an elementary physical education teacher. Although she did not coach as extensively as her husband, she was one of the best female athletes in the community, often winning local running races and tennis tournaments.

Both Mary and Dean grew up in the western part of the state, which was known for its majestic mountains and valleys and the once thriving coal mining industry. People from that part of the state were extremely loyal—especially with family—competitive, hardworking, and down to earth. So when Mary and Dean got married and moved to the south-central part of the state, they took those values with them and modeled and instilled them in their family, their students, and their players.

Penny's brothers made sure that she was always part of the games at the park. They were protective to a point, especially if some other guy tried to take advantage of the "girl playing sports with the boys." But beyond that, Penny was tackled and blocked in football like everyone else, expected to ice skate as fast as the boys, hit the tennis ball "like a man," and hit the golf ball as far or farther than anyone else.

And in the backyard of their home, Dean set up an exact replica of a softball pitching mound and home plate so that Penny could practice fast-pitch softball whenever there was a chance. Sometimes in the winter, Dean would clear the snow away on both the mound and the plate, and say, "Hey Pen, let's go throw a hundred or so pitches!" When there was too much snow, they would take a quick drive over to the high school gym and do the same: hundred or so pitches.

It was not surprising that Penny would become a standout scholar-athlete in high school and then in college as well. She often joked that, because her mother was a teacher in her elementary school and her dad was teacher-coach-athletic director during her high school years that she couldn't get in trouble if she wanted to—everybody knew her and, of course, her parents. It was also not surprising that she graduated from college with a teaching degree and was immediately hired by a school district near the one in which she grew up. What was a surprise was that her degree was in history!

She, of course, began coaching in her first year, and over the next decade she developed a reputation as an excellent teacher and coach. By the time she was thirty years old, she became the first female athletic director of the high school. And it never bothered her when people she would meet would say, "Oh, you're Dean's daughter, aren't you?"

Penny not only enjoyed coaching and teaching but also she was very interested in curriculum development and instructional design. She became involved in professional development activities, often being a presenter at local and regional professional development gatherings and conferences. By the age of thirty-five, she was enrolled in an educational leadership doctoral program and was named assistant principal of the high school that same year.

Within four years, she earned her doctorate and became the first female principal of the high school in which she worked. While some in the high school community—mostly men—were skeptical of a woman "running a comprehensive high school," her reputation as a leader was well established and the transition was very smooth for everyone.

Penny would remain the principal for eight years before being promoted to the position of assistant superintendent of Curriculum and Instruction. She was now forty-eight years old, never married, and like everything she learned growing up and experienced professionally, she had a wonderful work ethic, treated people with respect, was known to be an excellent listener and very collaborative, and used her competitive spirit and resolve to move the district's academic agenda forward.

She kept herself in excellent shape by jogging, playing tennis, and swimming all year round, went to church with her parents every Saturday night, and kept herself up to date by reading everything she could get her hands on that dealt with curriculum, instruction, student learning, and leadership.

Five years after accepting the position of assistant superintendent, Penny decided to apply for the superintendency in a nearby district. Her superintendent and the board president both wrote very positive letters of recommendation, as did the president of the teachers' union and the president of the district parent council. Penny prepared diligently for the application process, and to no one's surprise, she was invited for an initial interview with the board of education. She did an exemplary job in the interview, although she did notice that during the two-hour interview there were eight men and only one woman on the board, and that the woman had very little to say.

The board named Penny as one of the three finalists, with the next step being daylong interviews with groups of parents, teachers, community members, and administrators. There were a total of eight one-hour interviews during the day, followed by a dinner with the board in the evening. Once again, the only issue that concerned Penny was the lack of women not only on the board but within the ranks of administrative leadership as well. The two assistant superintendents were male, as were five of the six building principals.

Penny was offered the position and accepted it. Her family—especially her parents—was thrilled and proud of her. Things went well for Penny as superintendent during the first few years. She was able to lead the district in an overhaul of the K–12 curriculum and professional development for teachers. Her relationship with teachers and other administrators was generally positive.

Penny felt she had a good relationship with the board, although she was beginning to feel that when it came to issues such as finances, budget, buildings and grounds, and transportation, the board would often defer to Dennis, the assistant superintendent for Administrative Services and his department heads, who were all male. As a matter of fact, the board would often invite Dennis into executive session, and pretty much converse only with him, ignoring Penny.

It was in 2008 when the economy imploded and had devastating effects on businesses and organizations—including school districts—across the nation. Like other superintendents, Penny had to contend with uncertain times and fragile budgets. Yet at the same time, school districts were expected to continue to quest for all students reaching higher standards.

And so, when it was time for her to present the next budget, the board and public were shocked and dismayed. Penny recommended severe cuts in programs and layoffs of teaching and other personnel. The board began meeting on a weekly basis, often going into executive session to criticize Penny for her lack of leadership and then deferring to Dennis for his advice and plans.

A few weeks into this, Penny went to a regional superintendents' conference, titled "Providing Effective Leadership During Troubling Economic Times." The conference was scheduled for Friday through Sunday. During the Saturday session, Penny received a text from a colleague back in her district, saying, "Did you know the board met this morning about the budget and they invited Dennis to attend?" When she called the board president inquiring about this, his response was, "Well, you were out of town, and we really didn't want to bother you. On the other hand, I don't think it was very

wise of you to leave the district during this crisis. I certainly wouldn't have!"
He then hung up.

Penny remained at the conference, returning home on Sunday. The three-hour drive provided time for her to think about next steps. One thing she would not consider was quitting—she never has, and she never will. She would, however, meet with Dennis first thing on Monday and then ask to meet with the board in executive session during the upcoming meeting. And she would stop by later in the week to chat with her parents, who were still physically and mentally active, despite being in their late eighties. Penny had always considered both her father and mother as her mentors.

The meeting with Dennis on Monday was tense. In a very calm yet firm voice, Penny asked Dennis what the meeting was about, when he knew about the meeting, and why he didn't contacted her. Dennis responded that the meeting was about the finances and projected cuts in the upcoming budget that she had proposed. Dennis said that he was called late Friday by the board president about the meeting, which was to start the next morning at seven. He indicated it was too late to call that night and too early the next morning to call.

At this point, Penny raised her voice and said, "Have you ever heard of email? Texting? You work for me, not for the board! And if I ever find out that you have been meeting with board members without my knowledge, you can clean your desk out!"

She then called the board president and insisted on meeting with the board in executive session during the next board meeting, which was scheduled for two weeks from Wednesday. While he was not happy with Penny's demand, he said that, at least, he would poll the other members for their thoughts about the request. When he asked Penny the purpose of this request, in a very calm and polite manner, she responded, "I think you know very well what this is about."

It would take two days before the board president got back to Penny, stating, "The board majority is not looking very favorably at such a request when we are faced with this budget crisis, but they said they would listen to you."

During the next week, Penny and her staff continued to work on the budget, although she could feel the tension throughout the room, particularly between Dennis and her. She also felt that some of the other administrators were somewhat reluctant to share information, thoughts, and ideas. But Penny continued to ask for suggestions, debate pros and cons of proposed cuts, and so forth.

It was on Wednesday that she received a phone call from Rose DiPaolo, the only female member of the school board. Rose had been on the board for the past decade and was very quiet, calm, and for the most part voted with the majority on most issues. She was a staunch supporter of Penny's, but she never really spoke up. However, she did have a very strong following in the community since she was perceived as honest, hardworking, kind, and had students and teachers in the forefront of her service on the board.

Rose asked if Penny would be willing to meet with her for coffee on Saturday morning. Rose wanted this meeting to be just the two of them, and suggested a diner in a village about fifteen miles away. And Rose asked that Penny not share this with anyone, particularly the board president. Penny agreed, thinking to herself, "Wow, this is getting really weird!" Penny accepted the invitation, deciding to meet with Rose on Saturday and then her parents on Sunday afternoon.

On Saturday morning, Penny got up early and went jogging for about forty-five minutes. It was about 10:00 a.m. when she met with Rose at the diner. After exchanging pleasantries, Rose then said,

> I suppose you are wondering why I wanted to meet with you, particularly at this "far away place." You know, I've been on the board for ten years and still have another two years left. And then I was thinking of not running again. I'm almost seventy and don't know if I want to keep doing this.
>
> I've never been one to rock the boat. I think about things, see how it will help kids and teachers, and then make a decision on how I vote. And, by gosh, I was so happy when you became the superintendent. Finally, a woman! Maybe now, we can be kinder and really concentrate on teaching and learning. And try to do something about the "good old boys" on the board that run everything. I mean, it's the twenty-first century!

Penny listened intently, never expecting to hear this from Rose. And as she listened, she asked herself, where is this headed?

> The way they treat you and how they are doing things—well, I can't stand it! They are pulling the rug from out beneath you at every chance. The people that work directly for you are really working for them. They share everything with them, especially Dennis! Don't get me started. And it's all because you are a woman and as such, you are supposed to be second class.
>
> For a while, I thought it was just me. But then, a couple of weeks, when we were ending executive session, I heard two of the board members—one was the president—refer to you as a "bitch" and a very despicable term describing your sexuality. I cannot even repeat the term. I know you never married, but that's nobody's business. They didn't know I heard them, but I was appalled. And at that point, I decided that I was going to do something about this.
>
> So when I got to the "emergency meeting" on Saturday morning—and by the way, there was no emergency—and noticed you weren't present, it confirmed my worst fears. So, I'm here to tell you, that as of today, I will not step down in two years and I am going to work behind the scenes to let the community know what is going on. This meeting never happened. Just keep doing what you've been doing, and I'll take care of the rest. This crap stops now!

And with that, Rose stood up, put money on the table for the coffee, and left. Penny was stunned.

Two days later, Penny visited her parents for their usual Sunday afternoon dinner. They talked about politics, sports, the weather, and how other members of the family were doing. It was when they were sitting in the family room having coffee that Penny shared with her parents what had been taking place in the school district and what she had heard from the board member, Rose. As she was describing this, she noticed tears welling up in both her parents' eyes, something she had never seen before.

Penny: I am angry, confused and can't believe this is happening to me.

Father: You have every right to feel that way, and if you walked away from those idiots, I wouldn't blame you for a moment.

Penny: But both of you taught me from an early age to never quit . . . and I never have. That I was to stand up for myself.

Mother: But there are times when walking away might be the best thing to do. I don't want to see you quit, either. I wouldn't consider it quitting. At this point, you have to look at what this is doing to you, and whether or not you can continue to be effective or not. And the toll this will take on you both physically and emotionally.

Father: I know I can't, but I'd like to go over there and give them a piece of what they need!

Penny: What really hurts is that if I were a man, they wouldn't dare do this to me. I fought hard to get to the top of my profession—probably harder than men do. And then once I get there, they keep me out of the things that men are supposed to be doing! It's not right, and I won't stand for it!

Mother: Then I think we all know what you need to do.

Over the next week, Penny went about her job in her typical way. She was very professional and positive, especially around board members and administrators. Penny visited a number of schools to meet with teachers regarding the budget and possible consequences of the economic downturn. Penny wanted to make sure that no one would notice anything was amiss. Each evening, however, she wrote and rewrote what she was going to say to the board. She knew the key to this would be her ability to not be emotional, for if she was, this would certainly play into the hands of those on the board who used her gender against her.

The board meeting began on Wednesday evening, precisely at six. The meeting lasted for about three hours, as there was continued discussion of the budget and the usual agenda items that needed to be addressed. It was at about nine that the board president, in a rather dour voice, announced that the board would move into executive session for "personnel issues." He also stated that he did not expect any action to be taken after the session, and the board would likely adjourn for the evening.

Once the group was settled into another meeting room and the doors were closed, the board president turned to Penny and in a rather gruff manner said, "OK, you wanted this executive session . . . so what's this about?"

Penny had some notes in front of her but decided not to read anything, but to make eye contact with every member of the board as she spoke. She told herself to not blink, don't smile, be firm and be professional. And don't back down.

> First of all, I am not quitting. I am not going anywhere. And I haven't done anything to get myself fired. I have two-plus years left on my contract, and I expect to be here for that AND beyond.
>
> However, I will not tolerate what has been going on any further. First of all, since I am a woman, you have treated me like a second-class citizen. That I should only be involved with the curriculum and teaching stuff of the district, while the men in the district—both in this room and out there—get to deal with the men stuff: budgets, business, facilities, contracts, and so forth. By doing this, you have handcuffed me. You meet with members of my staff behind my back, call an "emergency" meeting when you know I am out of town, and who knows what else. This is wrong, and it needs to stop. And I will not let it keep happening. And as for my private life, it is none of your business. And if I ever hear demeaning words by any of you in this room toward my gender or who I am, you will be hearing from my lawyer!
>
> We are facing difficult times, as most districts are, considering what has happened to the economy.
>
> If we are to get through this, then we must work together. This will not work—and the public will know it's not working and why—if this continues. And let me repeat, I am not going anywhere. And I'm not changing who I am and how I do things. But I will not allow this board to pigeonhole me into what you think a female superintendent should be. How do you think the public will feel if they know this kind of behavior is occurring? What do you think will happen at the next election?
>
> I got to the superintendency by working hard—sometimes harder than others—by being ethical, collaborative, and with having the interests of children and teachers in the forefront of everything I have done and will continue to do. I wonder how many in here can say the same?
>
> We've got much work ahead of us. If you want to work with me, great. If not, then I move the district ahead without you. But I won't quit, and you will not box me into a corner ever again.
>
> Good evening.

Penny got up from her chair and left the room, in which there was not one sound coming from anyone.

Over the next months, Rose—true to her word—worked silently and diligently throughout the community, garnering support for Penny. She encouraged others to run for the board of education, and if not, to at least become more vocal and participatory at the board meetings.

Penny never again brought up what she had said to the board. She didn't have to. While there wasn't an immediate turn in how they treated her, over time some changes did occur. The board president decided not to run for another term the following spring, and two other members decided to step down at the time as well. Rose DiPaolo became president of the board, and Dennis, the assistant superintendent, took a position in another district.

The financial crisis would not go away for several years, and many districts like the one Penny was leading had to make huge budget cuts in both personnel and programs. Yet through it all, the district survived, and to many observers, it became better because of it. The district was able to demonstrate resiliency—being knocked down, getting back up, and being stronger. And nowhere within the district was this more evident than in their superintendent. Not many people knew what happened behind closed doors, but Penny was stronger and better for it, and as a result she was able to lead the district through these most difficult times and beyond!

LEARNING FOR LEADING

School leaders—particularly superintendents—face a more complex and mercurial environment than ever before. More accountability, less control, and the ever-present world of instant communication are just some of the daily issues facing such leaders. To some, surviving is just that—making it through the next day, week, or school year without being publicly humiliated or threatened with the loss of their job (or, in some cases, actually fired)! On the other hand, some thrive in this context. These leaders manage to move their districts (or schools) ahead in spite of the vortex in which they operate. Even when things go bad, these leaders seem to not only rebound but also in many cases actually become stronger! So why the difference?

Most positions of leadership require some basic preparation in terms of the (a) individual, (b) educational, and (c) experiential. School leaders—both superintendents and principals—are no different. Each of these types of preparation is unique and interrelated as well. Individual preparation can be defined in terms of the values, attitudes, and traits that an individual educator has in seeking a position of leadership. Examples of this include assertiveness in becoming a school leader or the reason one wants to become a school leader.

The second type of preparation is education, which can be defined in terms of the formal training and education in which an aspiring leader can become involved. In most cases, this preparation includes master's degrees, state-endorsed administrative certificate programs, and doctorate programs, most likely offered by colleges and universities.

The third type is experiential, in which the aspiring leader becomes involved in leadership through internships, beginning at lower-level leadership positions such as department chair/team leader and subsequently moving into higher levels of leadership, first at a school and then, perhaps, into central administrative positions.

Most likely, the assumption can be made that most, if not all, school leaders have had significant levels of these three types of preparation. And it can also be assumed that *not* everyone who has had such preparation will automatically be an exemplary school leader. Some find out during the application/interview process that perhaps this is not the direction they want to go in their professional life, while others may find out once they become a leader. Still others may find that they would have been better off remaining at the school level and not moving on to the central administration. Finally, some find that being the "assistant" is much more to their liking than being the "head."

Yet the focus here is on those leaders who want to be *the* leader of the school district or the school, have dutifully prepared, met the formal qualifications, and had the necessary experience. And they get to the top! But once they are there, they are treated differently to the extent that it is difficult or even impossible to succeed. And this often happens to those school leaders who might be one of the first to hold this leadership position. As the two stories from this chapter show, being the first female in a leadership position that has traditionally been held by a male can test the inner core of both the leader and the organization itself, leading to extreme stress for all involved—particularly the leader.

Contemporary school leaders are continually influenced by various social, political, and economic factors that exert pressures on their ability to not only lead the school (school district) but also to live a life that is personally and professionally safe and rewarding. However, a growing body of research has shown that school leaders, particularly superintendents, encounter considerable stress in their work, directly related to their roles and responsibilities of their position. Such stress among school leaders is increasing and can become "a disabling condition affecting behavior, judgment, and performance (Glass & Franceschini 2007, 47).[11]

It has been suggested that school superintendents, as leaders of their school districts, experience stress and strain in their occupations similar to that experienced by corporate executives. Research shows that school superintendents may even experience higher levels of stress than do other executives with respect to role overload and the level of responsibility (such as for the performance of building administrators, teachers, and students) that their position carries.

Findings from other studies have shown that sources of stress for school superintendents are multidimensional and include time pressures, a lack of communication and performance feedback, and conflicting demands of various constituencies. In addition, superintendents in large school districts and those who are younger and have fewer years of experience report higher levels of stress.

Because of the potential for high levels of debilitating distress as a result of the high levels of challenge and difficulty many superintendents experience in their jobs, their ability to cope effectively with the stress and overcome adversity becomes critical to their personal and professional success, and even their survival. Oftentimes superintendents, because of the considerable pressures they are under, tend to devote more time to managing the stress rather than focusing on the task of furthering the development of the school district. Effective coping strategies need to be put into place before the demands of the job overwhelm the executive's capability to carry out his or her responsibilities effectively.

People who cope successfully with the demands of their work and personal lives tend to possess and use cognitive dispositions that promote effective problem solving, engage in activities that help to reduce stress, and/or pursue social relationships that provide support in difficult times. All of these qualities and skills may moderate the potentially damaging effects of chronic stress, and a lack of such resources may amplify these effects.

A fair amount of research has identified resilience as a quality of individuals who cope effectively with stress, and Patterson and Kelleher (2005) suggest that effective school administrators exhibit resilient qualities. These qualities include the ability to assess the pertinent dimensions of problems that need to be addressed, holding strong beliefs in one's capacity to function effectively, and the understanding and energy to address problems effectively. Resilience is also viewed as a character trait that involves patience, responsibility, tolerance, and determination, as well as actions that focus on staying connected to others and taking care of one's emotional, spiritual, and physical development.

And so the question that should be addressed is, if stress has this impact across the board on superintendents and school leaders in general, to what extent might this affect those who become such educational leaders and are "first of their kind"? It is one thing, perhaps, to be an outsider brought in to assume a school leadership position, but it is quite different to be someone who may not look like the stereotypical leader.

As the two stories in this chapter illustrate, having successful coping skills can not only enable the educational leader to survive stressful occupational demands but also become even stronger as a person and professional as a result of successfully coping with a difficult situation or crisis. Being at the top of the pyramid can be very lonely, and it can make the school leader a very big target for an opponent. In the beginning of their book, *The Wounded Leader: How Real Leadership Emerges in Times of Crisis*, Ackerman and Maslin-Ostrowski (2002) submit:

> First, how does a reasonable, well-intentioned person, who happens to be a school leader, preserve a healthy and real sense of self in the face of a host of factors challenging that self in the best scenario, and leading to a wounding crisis in the worst? Second, what perspective toward the work of leadership might fortify the impact of these challenges, and produce a mind-set that leaves the person open to learn and grow from such experiences? [12]

During today's turbulent times, school leaders must be aware and be prepared for dealing with not only the sharks in the water that are visible but also those that cannot been seen. The educational environment today is more complex and volatile than ever, and school leaders—particularly superintendents—are more vulnerable to the whims of politics, to the pressure of the public, and employees seeking immediate answers, resolutions, and gratification within the tumultuous environment of contemporary technology.

Whereas a generation of school leaders before could take an afternoon off to relax and reflect while playing a round of golf or having an extended lunch with friends with little or any notice, in many communities, the school leader is expected to be accessible almost on a "24/7" basis!

And pity the school leader who makes a big mistake, an unpopular decision, or just has a run of bad luck. The sharks that were below water will now be swimming next to the others, waiting for their chance!

Thus, the question to be addressed is similar to that of Ackerman and Maslin-Ostrowski's: In today's educational context, how can a school leader survive *and* thrive? Of course, there are many who survive. And there are many who thrive. Yet how many are there that survive *and* thrive, such as Golda Meir and Penny Edwards did, in spite of the numerous obstacles they faced that perhaps others did not?

Throughout this book, a number of leaders have been presented who have had a laserlike focus on their core values and roots. Such leaders—both in and out of education—pay attention to and develop these values through their experiences, knowledge, and understanding of human nature and leadership. Why is it then that some leaders suffer deeply and others don't? Some thrive and others don't? Some survive and some don't? Some make a difference and some don't?

To some, the term *resiliency* means the ability of a person to get up after being knocked down. In the case of a school leader, it might be a principal who has a particularly bad year or so and is "put on notice" by the superintendent and school board. So the principal works hard at improving, and within a couple of years, she has regained her status and tenure as a principal.

However, to others, the term means much more than just "bouncing back" but actually emerging from misfortune and adversity stronger than before. Over the past several decades, a number of scholars such as Csikszentmihaly (1990) and Kahneman et al. (1999) have examined a practice within psychology referred to as *positive psychology*. This model is concerned with an emphasis on helping individuals to understand and develop personal strengths rather than correct weaknesses.

For example, positive psychology emphasizes personal experiences in terms of happiness and joy, positive character traits such as honesty, work ethic, and loyalty, and positive institutions such as families, neighborhoods, communities, and society as a whole. Using strategies from this concept, leaders can be motivated to learn, understand, and develop their own personal strengths.

However, resiliency and positive psychology most likely will not help a fallen leader if in fact this leader has not practiced, learned, and developed such ideas *prior* to the adversity striking. This type of learning takes much time and effort, yet regrettably, very few institutions who prepare and support aspiring and current school leaders spend a significant amount of time on concepts such as resiliency, the psychology of leaders, and "what do I do, as a school leader, when things go horribly wrong?" It is critical, therefore, that leaders at all stages of their career be cognizant of those practices that can provide a foundation to be successful, both during the good times and bad times.

Such success can be attributed not only to learning about and experiencing leadership, but more importantly, understanding and acting upon the nurturing, growth, and balance of who they are on inside and outside, in a manner that is sustainable. Based upon interviews with school leaders, observations of school leaders in action, personal experiences, and current literature, the following framework is offered in terms of how to "prepare for and weather the storm of school leadership" that every school leader will inevitably face, to one degree or another.

• *Physical Well-Being*: It is quite clear but often not so obvious to leaders that being in good physical shape is an important way to growth and sustainability. There is much research to strongly suggest that a school leader, working in an environment of stress, anxiety, and scrutiny, will be more likely to be resilient when they are physically fit because they have more stamina and focus. In addition, leaders who are involved in regular and intense physical fitness activities are less likely to be emotionally exhausted and burned out. In addition, such activities are likely to reduce anxiety, stress, and depression, and can increase feelings of alertness and vitality. Consider what one superintendent shared:

In the beginning, I didn't have time to work out. I was "too busy and too important." But then I began putting on weight, felt tired, and it began to have an impact on who I was. So, I just started walking and then, jogging. In the beginning, I would "fight all my battles" while I was walking or jogging. But what I discovered when I was finished is that I was emotionally and physically drained—and I hadn't gotten to work yet!

So then, when I jogged I listened to music, sometimes "classic rock," other times classical music. Then, I began to listen to books. I began to enjoy the time "away from the job" where I could just listen. No more fighting but just appreciating the experience. I lost some weight, began to feel better, began to eat better and I can't remember the last time I went to work feeling depressed, angry, and tired. I just wish I had started this a long time ago!

• *Emotional Well-Being*: The "roller-coaster ride" of school leadership is well documented. Test scores go up and everyone is happy! A state championship for a high school and "let the parades begin!" However, if there is bad news—a scandal involving inflated standardized test scores or the discovery of an inappropriate relationship between a teacher and a student—most likely many will be pointing the finger at the leader! As John F. Kennedy once said, "Victory has a thousand fathers, but defeat is an orphan!"

An emotionally healthy school leader is one who has inner peace with himself and others, which means that the leader will be less likely to allow himself to "get on the roller coaster" and be susceptible to the wild "ups and downs." Getting carried away with the enthusiasm of the celebratory events of when something great happens, or conversely, being dragged down when the news is bad, can have an overall negative impact on the leader, both personally and professionally.

Avoiding this "roller coaster" mentality is very difficult, particularly within the context of a society that values "wins and losses," "what have you done for us lately?" and action over inaction. This is not to suggest that the school leader be someone with no emotion—a straight line, but emotion that may fluctuate with the issues at hand—but not to a degree that will end up clouding judgment or even creating emotional reactions that are harmful to the leader and followers as well. As described below, emotional wellness includes the ability of the leader to be self-aware of his or her own emotions and practice healthy ways to observe and act in this ambiguous and uncertain world of school leadership.

I could not believe how well things were going in our district. Student achievement was increasing across all grades, bonds for new buildings were passed by the voters, and we had a new five-year contract with the teachers that everyone—yes everyone!—seemed to be pleased with.

Looking back, that's where the problem started. I was "Mr. Positive," who began to think I could do no wrong. Problems—big or small—I took care of them or had someone do it for me. I was riding high, and even began to look for bigger and better projects to get done in the district. Whatever I thought we needed, we did!

Before I knew it, hubris had set in. I was not looking at my leadership and the school district in a realistic manner. I certainly didn't have time to be reflective, and I wasn't listening to others. Literally, I was in the clouds of my leadership. And when things began to go wrong, the fall was swift and hurtful. And I didn't recover.

• *Intellectual Growth*: Children, it seems, are naturally curious about everything. From the bugs crawling around on the ground to the stars in the sky and everything in between, children wonder in awe as to what and why and how things are in the world in which they live. Being curious is a natural and critical part of human development, and for school leaders to be successful, they need to be as curious in this stage of their life, and perhaps even more than when they were young children.

For the argument can be made that asking questions and seeking answers are the foundation for intellectual growth in adults. For leaders, it is a critical skill to assess, evaluate, and make sound decisions on the difficult issues they face in their school district on a regular basis. Leaders need to adopt a more robust approach to problem solving, which is often dominated by a rational and linear approach. This includes questioning their own ideas and thoughts as well as those of others, and considering ideas from various perspectives.

For many school leaders, the opportunities to grow intellectually are rather limited. Many school leaders have a terminal degree, and if not, do not feel they have the time and resources to go back to a university to obtain a doctorate. School leaders have the opportunity to attend a conference or two each year, but the extent to which action occurs after new learning has been taken at these conferences can often be limited.

It is essential that school leaders remain as "lifelong learners," for several reasons. First, those who do are modeling this concept for other administrators, faculty, staff, and students in their school or district. In addition, the research is very clear that such intellectual stimulation actually helps adults to better retain, understand, and comprehend the world in which they live and lead. Researchers have concluded that as an adult gets older, the brain will become sharper the more it is used, particularly with higher-level thinking activities, including creative activities away from the job. Consider what this superintendent decided to do as he approached his sixty-fifth birthday:

> I knew I could retire in a couple of years and there was a part of me that wanted to. I kept asking myself, do I really want to keep doing this, especially in this environment that has swept through education. But I knew that I still had a lot to offer. So I talked with my wife and I said, I want to keep doing this until I reach fifty years in education, which is another seven years. I got my bachelor's degree in history, master's in administration, and doctorate in edu-

cational leadership, so my wife suggested that I go back and get a master's in something out of my comfort zone. We talked about it over time, and I decided that I would go back and get a master's degree in American Literature! And that's what I did!

For the next four years, there I was with in class with young adults learning about poetry and novels, drama and comedy. I was reading more than I had in years, and it was stuff so different from what I had been reading. And I was becoming much better at creative thinking and critical thinking, which certainly helped me as superintendent. More importantly, it helped me grow as a human. Next up: piano lessons!

• *Social Health*: Humans are social beings, in that an important part of growth and development is the extent to which individuals interact with others, including family, friends, neighbors, and colleagues. Being connected to others in a positive way helps to foster trust, commitment, and support for individuals to meet their potential, and perhaps beyond.

School leaders are no different. The days of being "the boss," who hovers over everyone, controls everyone, and is markedly distant from everyone, are over. Collaboration, consensus, and being transformational in leadership are in the forefront.

Yet as mentioned throughout this book, what the community says it wants from its school leader(s) and what it *really* wants can often be two different things, which can lead to role ambiguity for the school leader: the actual role and responsibilities of the school leader are vague and ill defined, expectations are unclear, and there is a level of uncertainty regarding consequences. While not every school leader faces such ambiguity, there is a considerable amount of research that suggests this is occurring more now than ever. Yet many school leaders lament the fact that "it's lonely at the top, especially during very difficult times."

Being connected with others can offer the school leader a network of social support that can help to alleviate the stress found within the context of contemporary education. For example, having a mentor or being a mentor is a proven way for the school leader to share thoughts and ideas, reflect upon situations, and take a look at what is occurring, from the vantage of seeing both the "trees and the forest" in a nonthreatening, nonevaluative manner.

Just as important to the leader's social health is the ability to be with friends and family away from the position. Having a core of friends to socialize with on a regular basis—whether it is going to dinner every month with friends, joining a running club, becoming a member of a civic club—can offer the leader a chance to do other significant activities that are not tied directly to their leadership position. Doing this will also help the leader fight against the need for their position as a school leader to be an all-consuming, "24/7" job!

Many of the school leaders interviewed, in fact, are involved in their own social well-being, and for many, it has been a part of their entire adult life. Others, on the other hand, realized the critical nature of this, and worked very hard at reconnecting with friends and colleagues or establishing new personal relationships.

However, there are some who, for different reasons, failed to take care of their social health, and ultimately, suffered the consequences. One superintendent shared the following:

> The longer I remained as superintendent in this district, the more distant I became. In our state, the superintendent is the only certificated member of the professional staff who cannot get tenure. So, all the principals, assistant principals, supervisors, directors, and assistant superintendents could all receive tenure. And these administrators had their own union as well. So automatically, there was a distance between me and them, even with those who were supposedly working right next to me on a daily basis. I understood this going into the job, but I really didn't care for this.
>
> So I didn't feel comfortable socializing with this group, other than the obligatory district celebratory events that take place throughout the year. Yet as things would get difficult, I began to shun away from not only them but my friends as well. I stopped golfing in the summer and skiing in the winter. If I went to dinner, it was usually only my wife and me. I didn't want to talk with anyone about what was going on.
>
> What a huge mistake. It was during these times that I needed to do things outside the office. Yet on one hand, I didn't want to share my thoughts, since to some it might appear to be a weakness. And so, my social life went down to almost nothing, I became somewhat of a social "recluse," and eventually, the quality of my leadership diminished.

• *Spiritual Well-Being*: This concept relates leadership to the awareness of a higher relevance, something that is beyond personal and professional goals. Having such a higher purpose forms a foundation for the individual to search for deeper meaning and intention of human existence, with the goal being the ability, in the case of school leaders, to strive for a state of harmony from within and for those being led.

Public school leaders are required by law to not bring formal religion into the schools that they lead, including but not limited to professional development faculty meetings. However, many school leaders have engaged in personal as well as group learning activities that emphasize value analysis, relaxation, and balancing one's inner needs with the rest of the world.

Over the past decade, the concept of mindfulness has emerged as a construct for leaders to help themselves and those they lead to become more aware of their thoughts, feelings, bodily sensations, and the immediate environment. With roots from Buddhist meditation, mindfulness is considered a more secular practice of individuals attempting to search for the deeper meaning of life and a state of personal harmony. Research has shown there are many benefits to practicing mindfulness, including lower blood pressure, improving social skills, less negative emotions, less symptoms of depression, and greater empathy and compassion.

Note what one principal said when she introduced the practice of mindfulness to her staff:

> At first they looked at me like I was crazy. But I told staff that this was not required, but those who wanted to try mindfulness could come to an after-school presentation.
>
> I brought in a speaker/trainer to the first session, and about ten teachers showed up. I didn't make a big deal, but we began to meet weekly. And pretty soon, some more teachers showed. The trainer stayed with us for the whole year.
>
> Of course, there was a little pushback from some, who said this was getting too religious. For me, this one hour a week really provided time to relax, reflect, and get rid of anxiety and guilt feelings. I began to see a change in how I dealt with others, especially during tense times. And others remarked similarly. When the school year ended, one of the teachers asked if we could do this with students!

• *Loving and Leading*: Brigadier General John H. Stanford was once asked to explain his philosophy of leadership. In a few short words, he stated, "Love 'em and lead 'em." Later, in an interview, leadership scholars James Kouzes and Barry Posner asked Stanford to elaborate. He said:

> I have the secret to leadership and life. The secret is to stay in love. Staying in love gives you the fire to really ignite other people, to see inside other people, to have a greater desire to get things done than other people. A person who is not in love doesn't feel the kind of excitement to get ahead and lead others and to achieve. I don't know any other fire, any other thing in life that is more exhilarating and is more positive a feeling than love is. [13]

The word *love* is often not associated with leadership. Yet in education, we hear of teachers "loving their students" and loving their school. But how often do we hear of a leader refer to followers in terms of love?

The word *love*, in this context, is not sensual but that of having a very deep and emotional level of caring for someone. One only needs to think back to "falling in love" for the first time, in which there was a sense of vulnerability, yet at the same time, a feeling of wanting to be with that person all of the time, of doing things for that person because it made this person feel good—and you as well—and that the other person's needs are of the highest priority.

Loving and leading starts with a natural feeling that the leader wants to serve the needs of the followers, first and foremost. Some consider this type of leader "inverting the pyramid" of traditional leadership. And in supporting the needs of followers, the leader's priority is listening, understanding, healing, supporting, and recognizing followers on a personal level, just as someone who is in love would.

A superintendent from a very large and very diverse school district with many needs explains how he was able to remain in that position for more than a decade when most of his colleagues in similar districts were most likely to leave within several years:

> Everywhere I went, every time I spoke, the word *love* was part of the conversation. At first, people thought maybe I wasn't sincere. But I was, and I was adamant about proving it.
>
> But that wasn't hard, because I always loved being in education: teacher, principal, superintendent. I mean, really loved it. Never thought of it as a job. Did I have bad days? Sure! But so did my wife and I, and yet we continue to love each other after forty-plus years of marriage.
>
> And that, I think was the key. When I was principal, I treated every student like they were my own children. Love them first and foremost. Same with the teachers, custodians, and so forth. Tell them all the time, "I love having you here with us" or "I love what you're doing." Shake hands, put an arm around someone, smile or cry with someone.
>
> You see, if you really love others, you feel much better about who you are as an individual. And that will help you be a much better leader!

Conclusion: Looking Back—and Ahead

Life is divided into three terms—that which was, which is, and which will be.
Let us learn from the past to profit by the present, and from the present, to live
better in the future.
—William Wordsworth[1]

One of the joys of life is a great story. Whether telling a story, listening to someone else tell a story, reading a story, or even viewing a story through a movie, there is something profound and poignant about a great story being told. Many of us, at one time or another, can remember sitting at the foot of a grandparent or an elderly neighbor who would provide us with a story from "way back when," told in the first person by someone who actually experienced a particular event of significance.

Stories can be funny or sad, simple or complex, short or long. Regardless, great stories stay with us. We learn from them, as we better understand who we are and who others are (or have been), as such stories can impart values, dreams, and life lessons. Yet in our world of instant communication, data and numbers, and "what have you done for me lately," it appears that telling stories and sharing history may be less significant. And sadly, education as it is today may be one of the biggest culprits.

With the emphasis on standards and accountability, school leaders are under much pressure to "just raise those test scores." And with that comes the inevitable standardization of curriculum and instruction and standardizing leadership. The only thing leaders are told to do regarding the past is to look at data over time, find the "root cause," make plans, and hope that such plans lead to higher test scores!

Leaders are more than analysts and managers! Yes, school leaders need the head (knowledge) of leadership and the hand (skills) of leadership, but also the heart of leadership! The heart of leadership is:

111

- Knowing who you are—from the inside out.
- Understanding who you serve.
- Being authentic.
- Willingness to share power.
- Encouraging community. It's not my school, my faculty, my students, my community; it's our school, our faculty, our students, our community.
- Expecting the best.
- Being courageous.
- Searching for wisdom.
- Being a role model.

And this is where history and stories converge in the development of a school leader. One cannot merely state, "As a school leader, I will do all of these things." To become such a leader, one must understand, experience, and practice such behaviors. And the starting point can be searching for, studying, and reading about exemplary historical leaders, as well as seeking opportunities to share his or her own stories and listen to the stories of others, which can be motivating and powerful leadership lessons.

Alas, searching for wisdom is that first step. And for exemplary leaders, it is not first step up that matters, or even getting to the top that matters; it's the steps heading down the mountain. For it is during this part of the leadership journey that learning, listening, sharing, and observing occur.

THE WISDOM OF THE MOUNTAIN

In ancient China, on top of Mount Ping, stood a temple where Hwan, the enlightened one, dwelled. Of his many disciples, we know only Lao-Li. For more than twenty years, Lao-Li studied and meditated under the great master. Although Lao-Li was one of the brightest and most determined disciples, he had yet to reach enlightenment. The wisdom of leadership was not his.

Lao-Li struggled with his lot for days, nights, months, even years. And then one day, the sight of a falling cherry blossom spoke to his heart. "I can no longer fight my destiny," he reflected. "Like the cherry blossom, I must gracefully resign myself to my ignorance." At that moment, after more than twenty years of study, Lao-Li decided to climb down the mountain and give up his hope of enlightenment.

Lao-Li searched for Hwan to inform him of his decision. He found the master sitting before a white wall, deep in meditation. Reverently, Lao-Li approached Hwan. "Excuse me, enlightened one," he said. But before Lao-Li could continue, the master spoke. "Tomorrow I will join you on your journey down the mountain," he said. And Lao-Li left to pack his belongings.

The next morning, before the descent, the master looked out into the vastness that surrounded the mountain peak where they stood. "Tell me, Lao-Li," he said. "What is it that you see?"

"Master, I see the sun beginning to wake just below the horizon. I see hills and mountains that go on for miles. In the valley I see an old town and a lake." Hwan listened to Lao-Li's response. He smiled and then took the first steps to start the descent.

Hour after hour, as the sun rose and crossed the sky, they walked. As they approached the foot of the mountain, Hwan again asked Lao-Li to tell him what he saw.

"Great wise one, in the distance I see roosters running round the barns, cows asleep in the flowering meadows, old people resting and children playing in a brook." The master stayed silent and walked to a large tree, where he sat at the trunk.

"What did you learn today Lao-Li?" he asked. Silence was Lao-Li's response. At last Hwan continued: "The road to leadership is like the journey down the mountain. It comes only to those who realize that what one sees at the top of the mountain is not what one sees at the bottom. Without this wisdom, we close our minds to all that we cannot view from our position and as a consequence limit our capacity to grow and improve. But with wisdom there comes an awakening. We recognize that alone one sees only so much—which, in truth, is not much at all. This is the wisdom that opens our minds to improvement, knocks down prejudices, and teaches us to respect what at first we cannot view. Never forget this last lesson, Lao-Li: What you cannot see can be seen from a different part of the mountain."

When the master stopped speaking, Lao-Li looked out at the horizon, and as the sun set before him it seemed to rise in his heart. Lao-Li turned to the master, but the great one was gone.

—Ancient Chinese Leadership Parable

Great school leaders are aware of the past and the present. But to understand the past and the present, they also must be self-aware. Whatever their mission in school leadership is, they value themselves in terms of their own strengths, challenges, and beliefs—just as all great leaders from the past have. They will adapt to an ever-changing world, just as all great leaders from the past have. They engage those around them by inspiring and challenging others—just like great leaders from the past have. And they will energize themselves and others by having a desire for success for the greater good—just like great leaders from the past have. We don't have to look too far to figure out what great school leadership looks like. History and stories are a great starting point!

Bibliography

Ackerman, R. & Maslin-Ostrowski, P. (2002). *The Wounded Leader*. San Francisco: Jossey Bass.

Baum, L. Frank. (1900). *The Wonderful Wizard of Oz*. Chicago: Aristeus Books.

Berg, A. Scott. (2013). *Wilson*. New York: G. P. Putnam's Sons.

Bolman, L. & Deal, T. (2006). *The Wizard and the Warrior: Leading with Passion and Power*. San Francisco: Jossey Bass.

Bolman, L. & Deal, T. (2011). *Leading with Soul: An Uncommon Journey of Spirit* (3rd ed.). San Francisco: Jossey-Bass.

Brunner, C. & Grogan, M. (2007). *Women Leading School Systems*. Lanham, MD: Rowman & Littlefield.

Collins, J. (2001). *Good to Great: Why Some Companies Make the Leap . . . and Others Don't*. New York: Harper Business.

Council of the Great City Schools. (2014). *Urban School Superintendents: Characteristics, Tenure, and Salary: Eighth Survey Report*. Washington: Author.

Covey, S. (1989). *The 7 Habits of Highly Effective People*. New York: Simon & Schuster.

Covey, S. (1990). *Principle-Centered Leadership*. New York: Simon & Schuster.

Covey, S. (2004). *The 8th Habit: From Effectiveness to Greatness*. New York: Simon & Schuster.

Csikszentmihaly, M. (1990). *Flow*. New York: Harper & Row.

Dana, J. & Bourisaw, D. (2006). *Women in the Superintendency*. Lanham, MD: Rowman & Littlefield Education.

Deal, T. & Peterson, K. (2009). *Shaping School Culture: Pitfalls, Paradoxes, and Promises* (2nd ed.). San Francisco: Jossey-Bass.

Dewey, J. (1933). *How We Think: A Restatement of the Relation of Reflective Thinking to the Educative Process*. Boston, MA: Heath.

Divya, J. (2002). *Gandhi on Khadi*. Mumbai: Mouj Printing Bureau.

Eliot, T. S. (1943, 1971). *Four Quartets*. Orlando, FL: Harcourt.

Evans, R. (1996). *The Human Side of School Change: Reform, Resistance, and the Real-Life Problems of Innovation*. San Francisco: Jossey-Bass.

Fullan, M. (2008). *The Six Secrets of Change*. San Francisco: Jossey-Bass.

Glass, T., Bjork, L., & Brunner, C. (2000). *The Study of the American School Superintendency, 2000: A Look at the Superintendent in the New Millennium*. Arlington, VA: American Association of School Administrators.

Glass, T. & Franceschini, L. (2007). *The State of the American School Superintendency: A Mid-Decade Study*. Lanham, MD: Rowman & Littlefield.

Goldring, R., Gray, L., & Bitterman, A. (2013). *Characteristics of Public and Private Elementary and Secondary School Teachers in the United States: Results from the 2011–12 Schools and Staffing Survey* (NCES 2013-314). U.S. Department of Education. Washington, DC: National Center for Education Statistics.

Goodwin, D. (1994). *No Ordinary Time: Franklin and Eleanor Roosevelt—The Home Front in World War II*. New York: Simon & Schuster, Inc.

Gosling, J. & Mintzberg, H. (2003). The Five Minds of a Manager. *Harvard Business Review* 81(11): 54–64.

Harvey, J. (1988). *The Abilene Paradox and Other Meditations on Management*. Lexington, MA: Lexington Books.

Herman, A. (2008). *Gandhi & Churchill: The Epic Rivalry That Destroyed an Empire and Forged Our Age*. New York: Bantam Dell.

Huttenback, R. (1971). *Gandhi in South Africa*. Ithaca, NY: Cornell University Press.

Kahneman, E., Diener, E., & Schwarz, N. (1999). *Well-Being: Foundations of Hedonic Psychology*. New York: Russell Sage Foundation.

Katz, S. (2004). Women School Superintendents: Perceptions of Best Practices for Leadership. *Journal of Women in Educational Leadership* 2(3): 155–80.

Kipling, R. (2008). *Collected Works of Rudyard Kipling, Volume 1*. Charleston, SC: BiblioBazaar.

Kolb, D. (1984). *Experiential Learning: Experience as the Source of Learning and Development*. Englewood Cliffs, NJ: Prentice-Hall.

Kotter, J. (2012). *Leading Change*. Boston: Harvard Business Review Press.

Kouzes, J. & Posner, B. (1992). Ethical Leaders: An Essay About Being in Love. *Journal of Business Ethics* (11)5: 479–84.

Kouzes, J. & Posner, B. (2012). *The Leadership Challenge: How to Make Extraordinary Things Happen in Organizations*. San Francisco: Jossey-Bass.

Kowalski, J., McCord, R., Petersen, G., Young, P., & Ellerson, N. (2011). *The American School Superintendent: 2010 Decennial Study*. Lanham, MD: Rowman & Littlefield.

Litchka, P., Fenzel, M., & Polka, W. (2009). The Stress Process Among School Superintendents. *International Journal of Educational Leadership Preparation* 4(4). MacGregor Burns, J. (1978). *Leadership*. New York: Harper & Row Publishers.

Machiavelli, N. (2003). *The Prince and Other Writings*, Wayne Rebhorn (trans.). New York: Barnes and Noble Classics.

Mango, A. (1999). *Ataturk: The Biography of the Founder of Modern Turkey*. New York: Overlook Press.

McGee Banks, C. (2007). Gender and Race as Factors in Educational Leadership and Administration. In M. Grogan & M. Fullan, *The Jossey-Bass Reader on Educational Leadership* (2nd ed.). San Francisco: Jossey-Bass.

Medzini, M. (2008). Israel's Midwife: Golda Meir in the Closing Years of the British Mandate. *Israel Affairs* (14)3.

Meir, G. (1975). *My Life*. London: Cox and Wyman.

Miller, L. (1984). *American Spirit: Visions of a New Corporate Culture*. New York: Morrow.

Patterson, J. & Kelleher, P. (2005). *Resilient School Leaders*. Alexandria, VA: ASCD.

Polka, W. & Litchka, P. (2008). *The Dark Side of Educational Leadership: Superintendents and the Professional Victim Syndrome*. Lanham, MD: Rowman & Littlefield.

Raelin, J. & Coghlan, D. (2006). Developing Managers as Learners and Researchers: Using Action Learning and Action Research. *Journal of Management Education* 30(5): 670–89.

Schein, E. (2010). *Organizational Culture and Leadership* (4th ed.). San Francisco: Jossey-Bass.

Schön, D. (1983). *The Reflective Practitioner: How Professionals Think in Action*. New York: Basic Books.

Tichy, N. & Devanna, M. A. (1990). *The Transformational Leader*. New York: John Wiley & Sons.

Tomalin, C. (2011). *Charles Dickens: A Life*. New York: Penguin Press.

Triger, Z. (2014). Golda Meir's Reluctant Feminism: The Pre-State Years. *Israel Studies* (19)3.

United States Department of Education, National Center for Education Statistics. (2011–2012). *Racial/Ethnic Enrollment in Public Schools Report.*

United States Department of Education, National Center for Education Statistics. (2013). *School Staffing Report: 2011–12.* Washington, DC: Author.

Wheatley, M. (2006). *Leadership and the New Science.* San Francisco: Berrett-Koehler, Inc., 147.

Wheatley, M. (2012). *So Far from Home: Lost and F o und in our Brave New World.* San Francisco: Berrett-Koehler Publishers.

William Wordsworth Quotes. Quotes.net. http://www.quotes.net/quote/6067.

Notes

PREFACE

1. For this book, *school leader(s)* will generally be used to refer to being a superintendent of schools or the principal of a school.
2. R. Kipling, *Collected Works of Rudyard Kipling, Volume 1* (Charleston, SC: BiblioBazaar, 2008).
3. Author's note: For the stories found in the book, pseudonyms have been used to protect the anonymity of each school leader, and the names of specific locations have been changed as well.

1. *TEMET NOSCE* (KNOW THYSELF)

1. S. Covey, *Principle-Centered Leadership* (New York: Free Press, 1990).
2. J. Kouzes and B. Posner, *The Leadership Challenge*, 5th ed. (San Francisco: Jossey-Bass, 2012).
3. L. Bolman and T. Deal, *Leading with Soul: An Uncommon Journey of Spirit* (3rd ed.) (San Francisco: Jossey-Bass, 2011), 9.
4. Ibid., 198.
5. A. Scott Berg, *Wilson* (New York: G. P. Putnam's Sons, 2013), 202–3.
6. Ibid., 207.
7. Ibid., 211.

2. THE MAGIC BEHIND THE MEANING

1. L. Frank Baum, *The Wonderful Wizard of Oz* (Chicago: Aristeus Books, 1990), 72.
2. US Department of Education, National Center for Education Statistics, *School Staffing Report: 2011–12* (Washington, DC: Author, 2013).
3. US Department of Education, National Center for Education Statistics, *Racial/Ethnic Enrollment in Public Schools Report 2011–2012.*

4. L. Bolman and T. Deal, *Wizard and the Warrior: Leading with Passion and Power* (San Francisco: Jossey Bass, 2006), 89–90.

5. E. Schein, *Organizational Culture and Leadership* (4th ed.) (San Francisco: Jossey-Bass), 236.

6. Ibid., 237.

7. T. Deal and K. Peterson, *Shaping School Culture: Pitfalls, Paradoxes, and Promises* (2nd ed.) (San Francisco: Jossey-Bass, 2009), 15.

8. Ibid., 200.

9. A. Mango, *Ataturk: The Biography of the Founder of Modern Turkey* (New York: Overlook Press, 1999), 434.

10. J. Divya, *Gandhi on Khadi* (Mumbai: Mouj Printing Bureau, 2002), 32.

11. Ibid., 57.

12. Ibid., 47.

13. A. Herman, *Gandhi and Churchill: The Epic Rivalry That Destroyed an Empire and Forged Our Age* (New York: Bantam Dell, 2008), 359.

14. L. Miller, *American Spirit: Visions of a New Corporate Culture* (New York: Morrow, 1984), 54–55.

3. FROM CHRYSALIS TO BUTTERFLY

1. N. Machiavelli, *The Prince and Other Writings*, Wayne Rebhorn (trans.) (New York: Barnes and Noble Classics, 2003), 25.

2. J. MacGregor Burns, *Leadership* (New York: Harper & Row Publishers, 1978), 20.

3. N. Tichy and M. Devanna, *The Transformational Leader* (New York: John Wiley & Sons, 1990), 5–6.

4. J. Kouzes and B. Posner, *The Leadership Challenge: How to Make Extraordinary Things Happen in Organizations* (San Francisco: Jossey-Bass, 2012), 209.

5. R. Evans, *The Human Side of Change: Reform, Resistance, and the Real-Life Problems of Innovation* (San Francisco: Jossey-Bass, 1996), 39.

6. J. Kotter, *Leading Change* (Boston: Harvard Business Review Press, 2012), 27.

7. Ibid., 34.

8. M. Fullan, *The Six Secrets of Change* (San Francisco: Jossey-Bass, 2008), 52.

9. R. Huttenback, *Gandhi in South Africa* (Ithaca, NY: Cornell University Press, 1971), 163.

10. Ibid., 168.

11. J. Harvey, *The Abilene Paradox and Other Meditations on Management* (Lexington, MA: Lexington Books, 1988).

4. THINKING ABOUT THINKING

1. J. Gosling and H. Mintzberg, "The Five Minds of a Manager," *Harvard Business Review* 81, no. 11 (2003): 54–64.

2. Ibid., 58.

3. M. Wheatley, *Leadership and the New Science* (San Francisco: Berrett-Koehler Inc., 2006), 147.

4. J. Dewey, *How We Think: A Restatement of the Relation of Reflective Thinking to the Educative Process* (Boston, MA: Heath, 1933), 14.

5. Ibid., 21.

6. J. Raelin and D. Coghlan, "Developing Managers as Learners and Researchers: Using Action Learning and Action Research," *Journal of Management Education* 30, no. 5 (2006): 670–89.

7. C. Tomalin, *Charles Dickens: A Life* (New York: Penguin Press, 2011), 148–49.
8. T. S. Eliot, *Four Quartets* (Orlando, FL: Harcourt, 1943, 1971), 27.
9. M. Wheatley, *So Far from Home: Lost and Found in our Brave New World* (San Francisco: Berrett-Koehler Publishers, 2012), 130–31.
10. Ibid., 143.

5. SURVIVING AND THRIVING

1. D. Goodwin, *No Ordinary Time: Franklin and Eleanor Roosevelt—The Home Front in World War II* (New York: Simon & Schuster, Inc., 1994), 208.
2. Council of the Great City Schools, *Urban School Superintendents: Characteristics, Tenure, and Salary: Eighth Survey Report* (Washington: Author, 2014).
3. J. Kowalski, R. McCord, G. Petersen, P. Young, and N. Elverson, *The American School Superintendent: 2010 Decennial Study* (Lanham, MD: Rowman & Littlefield, 2011).
4. R. Goldring, L. Gray, and A. Bitterman, *Characteristics of Public and Private Elementary and Secondary School Teachers in the United States: Results from the 2011–12 Schools and Staffing Survey (NCES 2013-314)*. U.S. Department of Education (Washington, DC: National Center for Education Statistics, 2013). http://nces.ed.gov/pubsearch.
5. C. McGee Banks, "Gender and Race as Factors in Educational Leadership and Administration." In *Jossey-Bass Reader on Educational Leadership* (2nd ed.) (San Francisco: Jossey-Bass, 2007), 317.
6. Z. Triger, "Golda Meir's Reluctant Feminism: The Pre-State Years," *Israel Studies* 19, no. 3 (2014): 127.
7. M. Medzini, "Israel's Midwife: Golda Meir in the Closing Years of the British Mandate," *Israel Affairs* 14, no. 3 (2008): 397.
8. US Department of Education, National Center for Education Statistics, *School Staffing Report: 2011–12* (Washington, DC: Author, 2013).
9. G. Meir, *My Life* (London: Cox and Wyman, 1975), 114.
10. Ibid., 103.
11. T. Glass and L. Franceschini, *The State of the American School Superintendency: A Mid-Decade Study* (Lanham, MD: Rowman & Littlefield, 2007).
12. R. Ackerman and P. Maslin-Ostrowski, *The Wounded Leader* (San Francisco: Jossey-Bass, 2002), xi.
13. J. Kouzes and B. Posner, "Ethical Leaders: An Essay About Being in Love," *Journal of Business Ethics* 11, no. 5 (1992): 479–84.

CONCLUSION: LOOKING BACK—AND AHEAD

1. William Wordsworth Quotes. Quotes.net. http://www.quotes.net/quote/6067.

About the Author

Peter (Pete) Litchka is associate professor of Education and director of the Educational Leadership Program at Loyola University Maryland. Prior to arriving at Loyola University Maryland, Pete spent more than thirty years in public education as a teacher, coach, school administrator, assistant superintendent, and superintendent of schools (twice). He has a bachelor's degree from the State University of New York at Geneseo, a master's from Johns Hopkins University, and a doctorate from Seton Hall University.

Pete has been recognized at the local, state, and national levels for his contributions to education. He was a teacher-of-the-year in Maryland, received the Milken National Educator Award, the Foundation for Teaching Economics National Award for Excellence in Economic Education, and received three state awards for curriculum by the Maryland Council for Economic Education.

Since arriving at Loyola University Maryland in 2006, Pete has presented research in more than fifty conferences in the United States as well as in Cyprus, Israel, Poland, and Turkey. He has coauthored two books: *Living on the Horns of Dilemmas: Superintendents, Politics, and Decision-Making* (2014) with Walt Polka and Frank Calzi, and *The Dark Side of Educational Leadership: Superintendents and the Professional Victim Syndrome* (2008) with Walt Polka. Pete has had numerous articles published in peer-review leadership journals both in the United States and abroad.

In addition, Pete has served as a consultant to a number of schools and school districts in leadership development and school improvement.

He currently resides with his wife, Isabella, and dog, Shilah, in Hunt Valley, Maryland.

www.ingramcontent.com/pod-product-compliance
Lightning Source LLC
Chambersburg PA
CBHW021602210326
41599CB00010B/560